To

Elsie Gibbs

With love and appreciation
for your devoted service
and fine Christian Fellowship
in the Woman's Society
of Christian Service of
Fairfield First Methodist Church.

Sept. 20, 1956

THE
MATURE HEART

Helen B. Emmons

THE
MATURE HEART

New York • ABINGDON PRESS • Nashville

THE MATURE HEART

Copyright MCMLIII by Pierce & Washabaugh

Library of Congress Catalog Card Number: 53-5394

242

B
SET UP, PRINTED, AND BOUND BY THE
PARTHENON PRESS, AT NASHVILLE,
TENNESSEE, UNITED STATES OF AMERICA

Foreword

LIFE IS GOOD when spiritual growth keeps pace with the years. To be able to "trust God, see all, nor be afraid" puts a bird's song in the heart. Life is good when its losses are balanced by a compensating enrichment of the heart.

The purpose of this volume is to offer suggestions for the enrichment of the heart. It would explore ways in which we may live in harmony with the conditions which surround us, and in harmony with the Spirit of God within us. It would point out ways of awareness of the presence of God, of courageous acceptance of what life brings, and of radiant hope of a greater life beyond the one we now know. It would show also ways of joyous service to our fellow men.

The meditations are arranged in a progressive order of topics so that you may read them consecutively, a page at a time. But if you prefer to select according to the need of the moment, the index will help you find the meditation to suit the time. (Note especially the meditations for five special days at the back of the book.) A quiet spot where you can be alone with God opens the way for hearing His voice. Yet God may speak also through loved ones when you can share a time of devotion with those who care to think together about the personal applications of His Word. It will be best to read first in your Bible the passage suggested at the head of the page, then ponder the truth expressed in the text as you have discovered it in your own experience. The prayer at the end of each meditation has

5

been left unfinished, for it is intended to be only a beginning for your own praying.

Grateful acknowledgment is due *The Upper Room* for permission to use adaptations of several meditations of mine originally printed there. Also, acknowledgment should be made that I have followed the pattern and style of *The Upper Room*, because of its excellence as well as its familiarity to me. In the early days of *The Upper Room* it was my privilege to share in the editing of this devotional magazine, which was founded and for ten years edited by my late husband, Grover Carlton Emmons.

A list of sources is given at the back of the book. I am grateful to the copyright owners who have given me permission to quote selections. I wish that sources could be listed for many which I have been unable to trace. For forty years I have collected bits of poetry, stories, and inspiring thoughts to use in Sunday-school lessons and in other devotional talks. At the time I did not think that I might wish to include them in a book.

My daughter, Mary Emmons Worthington, has been of great help to me by her typing of the manuscript.

HELEN B. EMMONS

Contents

I. Cultivating Spiritual Values

II. Living Victoriously

III. Self-Giving

IV. Trusting the Unseen

V. Special Days

CONTENTS

God's Music

The heavens declare the glory of God.—Ps. 19:1

God is at the organ;
  I can hear
A mighty music echoing,
  Far and near.

—EGBERT SANDFORD

GOD'S MUSIC is in our ears everywhere in his beautiful world. We hear it in hurrying streams, sighing winds, singing birds, falling waters, and lapping waves. But deeper still we hear it in our hearts when we stop to listen. It comes in martial strains calling us to work and to the service of our fellow men. It comes in softer melody calling us to rest and contemplation. Again it comes in triumphant strains from another world when the gates open and loved ones enter in.

There is always singing about us. But we get so engrossed in the noise around us that we fail to hear it. We listen to the strife and sorrow in the world. We forget to listen for the music of the permanent values, the things that are right and true.

There is music in a mother's love, a child's trust, a happy home, a brave man's battle for a better world, an unselfish act, a kindly deed. There is "a mighty music echoing, far and near."

God of all music, tune my heart to listen for Thy voice in all Thy creation.

Look for Something Beautiful

He hath made everything beautiful in his time. —Eccl. 3:11

ALICE FREEMAN PALMER, one-time president of Wellesley College, taught a class of tenement children every Sunday morning. A pale, thin child, who was always carrying a heavy baby, came to her class.

One day the child asked her teacher, "Can you tell us how to be happy?"

Searching for an answer to the child's need, Mrs. Palmer said, "Look for something beautiful every day this week and tell me what you found next Sunday."

The child returned and reported the beautiful things she had discovered.

"But one day it rained," she said, "and I could not take the baby out to look for something beautiful. Then the sun came out, and I saw it shine on the baby's hair."

Look for something beautiful each day. It may be found even in a heavy burden from which we cannot escape. It is not always the large, important things which bring happiness. Little things which surround us often bring the truest joy. The gold of a baby's hair, a lovely flower, firelight on the floor, a loving smile can make our hearts sing. They are signs of our Father's love and care for us.

Give me, O Father, an appreciation for the countless joys which surround me every day. Let me find Thy beauty in hidden places.

10

Seeing the Invisible

In the year that King Uzziah died, I saw also the Lord sitting upon a throne, high and lifted up, and his train filled the temple.

—Isa. 6:1

ROBINSON CRUSOE tracked his lonely and presumably uninhabited island day after day. Suddenly one day he saw the imprint of a human foot upon the sandy shore. His life was never the same from that moment. His whole idea of the island was different. All his plans were changed. His world was transformed.

Someone has said that it is what a man sees in life that either makes or unmakes him. A man walks on the hilltops of life or trudges through the valleys depending on what he sees. Isaiah said, "Mine eyes have seen the King," and proclaimed God's message in an era of crisis. Moses saw a bush aflame with divinity and led his people out of bondage. Saul of Tarsus saw Jesus on the Damascus road and broke forth with a gospel for all the world. David Livingstone had a vision of light and threw that light across darkest Africa.

What a man sees in himself determines whether or not God can use him to bless his fellow men. When he sees his own unworthiness matched by the power of God, he is ready to be used. Humbly he seeks the opportunity God offers him, saying, "Here am I; send me."

Help me to see Thee, my Father, and to consecrate myself to serve in ways Thou dost open before me.

11

Riches of the Heart

Set your affection on things above, not on things on the earth.
—Col. 3:2

THERE IS A LEGEND of a boy who ran away from home to see the world. When he started out he picked up bright pieces of glass, smooth round pebbles, and bird nests, and put them into a sack on his back. As the day wore on, the sack grew so heavy that the boy had to sort out his treasures and discard some of them. Gradually he gave them all up. When he returned home at night, he was as empty-handed as when he left in the morning.

This is a parable of our life upon earth. We come into it with empty hands and leave it with empty hands. The material things we acquire through the years are left behind at the end. We take with us only our spiritual riches. Beauties of character, friendships, treasures of mind and soul—these belong to us forever. "The things which are seen are temporal; but the things which are not seen are eternal."

Jesus had only a little to call his own of earthly possessions. But he showed his appreciation of all good and lovely things. He had more to give than any other person. His life overflowed with love and mercy. His were the true riches.

Heavenly Father, correct my sense of values. Set my heart on the riches that endure.

Values That Cannot Be Lost

Giving thanks always for all things unto God the Father in the name of our Lord Jesus Christ. —Eph. 5:20

WHEN MY DAUGHTER was three, she received her first straw hat from her grandmother, at whose home we were visiting. It meant to her the putting away of baby bonnets and the beginning of girlhood. We stood by the rail of the ferry crossing San Francisco Bay on our homeward journey. A puff of a breeze carried the little hat over the water. There was no recovery. That night as she knelt to pray, she said, "Let's thank God for my new hat—but let's not tell Him we lost it!"

Life has many losses. It is easy to mourn over them and to dwell on our misfortune. But is it not better to thank God for the joy we had in possessing our treasures for a time? Remembrance is a comfort when we think on this joy rather than on the sorrow of loss.

Material things do not last. But spiritual blessings are eternal, and no circumstance or person can take them away from us. The wind may blow away a hat, but it cannot blow away what the hat has meant to the heart. If we find the spiritual value in each material gift, we can never lose it. Regardless of what happens, we can keep on "giving thanks always for all things unto God."

Gracious Lord, help me to remember the eternal values in all I have loved and lost, that I may always give Thee thanks.

Read Ps. 84

Choose the Lee Side

O Lord of hosts, blessed is the man that trusteth in thee.
—Ps. 84:12

SANTA CATALINA ISLAND lies twenty-one miles off the coast of Southern California. The windward side of the island faces the open sea and is swept by gales. The shore line is bare and rocky. The lee side of the island is warm and sunny. Lovely homes dot the sheltered mountainsides. Beautiful Avalon Bay is covered with pleasure craft. Glass-bottom boats reveal the blue depths of the quiet waters.

Life has a windward side and a lee side. The average person lives on the windward side. His life is exposed to all the storms that rise. Disappointments shatter his dreams; sorrows overwhelm his heart; fears destroy his hope. He is lonely of heart.

The Christian lives on the lee side of life. He is protected from life's blows because he has the consciousness of God's care around him. His heart is at peace and reflects the face of his Father in its quiet depths. He delights in the beauty of the world about him. He finds joy in the companionship of God's children. He rejoices in the hope of eternal life.

Everyone may choose which side of life he will live on. No other can make the choice for him.

My Father, I choose to live with Thee in this life and in the world to come.

Quietness

In quietness and in confidence shall be your strength.
— Isa. 30:15

THE HALL OF the Crucifixion in Forest Lawn Memorial Park was built to house the painting of the crucifixion by Jan Styka, a Polish artist. It was brought to this country in 1900, but not exhibited until 1944. No gallery in Europe was large enough to hang it. It is a painting one hundred and ninety-five feet long, and forty-five feet high.

The doors of the building are opened on each hour during the afternoon. You find yourself in a vast amphitheater, dimly lighted. You remain in stillness for fifteen minutes. Then the curtains are withdrawn to reveal the majestic panorama. The period of silence is needed to prepare the mind and heart for the great experience.

God speaks to men of quiet hearts. His voice is heard when there is calmness and stillness of spirit.

It is possible to cultivate a quiet spirit even in a loud and busy world. When you refuse to be hurried or distracted by the confusion of life, you are able to draw upon God's power. You are able, in the words of Edward H. Griggs, to "stand in the midst of darkness and live as though all about you were light."

Holy Father, I will be still and know that Thou art God. Give me a quiet heart.

Serenity

Thou wilt keep him in perfect peace, whose mind is stayed on thee; because he trusteth in thee. —Isa. 26:3

IN A LETTER dated December 22, 1951, E. Stanley Jones writes: "As the years come and go I feel less and less that I'm doing things. I'm just letting God do things through me. And it all seems so effortless and non-fatiguing. The strain and hence the drain are gone. The years glide into each other as the new cars pick up higher gears, without noise and apparently without effort. Life is beautiful—in Him."

The word "serene" sometimes is used in speaking of persons of exalted rank. A prince may be spoken of as "His Serene Highness." He is assumed to have a calm radiance above his fellows. More often the word denotes quietness, as of a placid lake or a blue and cloudless sky.

A serene spirit comes with maturity of heart. Someone said of a woman who has had repeated misfortunes, "No matter what happens to her, she goes serenely on her way." This woman's heart is quiet because God dwells there. She feels her joys to be greater than her losses. She prays for guidance each day. She does what she feels God wants her to do. She leaves the future in His hands.

Dear Lord, help me to put my trust in Thee. Give me a serene spirit which rests in Thee.

Solitude

I am not alone, because the Father is with me.—John 16:32

MOSES TENDING SHEEP alone in the desert met God in the burning bush. Elijah hiding alone in a cave heard God's call to unfinished tasks. Jesus alone for forty days in the wilderness found God's plan for his life.

All of us need periods of withdrawal from other people. Great things are accomplished in the depths of what we sometimes call loneliness. Out of it come poise, serenity, faith, and vision. We should welcome solitude as a sanctuary.

> Your loneliness is a cathedral.
> You are the priest.
> You are the congregation.
> You are the choir and the organ.
> You are the music.
> You are the altar and
> The white burning candles
> And their yellow light.
> Your solitude is multitude;
> A cloud of witnesses surrounds you;
> The Lord of Hosts encompasses you.
> Your solitude is multitude.
> Your solitude is a cathedral.
>
> —AUTHOR UNKNOWN

Deliver me, my Father, from the fear of loneliness. Make my hours of solitude bright with Thy presence.

Thou Art the Christ!

He saith unto them, But who say ye that I am? And Simon Peter answered and said, Thou art the Christ, the Son of the living God. —Matt. 16:15-16

WILLIAM HAZLITT wrote a little essay called "Of Persons One Would Wish to Have Seen." It is the story of a conversation between Charles Lamb and a group of friends in London about persons they would like to have met. Many names were mentioned, including Chaucer, Dante, Pope, Oliver Cromwell, and others.

"There is only one other person," Lamb said finally. "If Shakespeare was to come into the room, we should all rise up to meet him; but if that person was to come into it, we should all fall down and try to kiss the hem of his garment!"

When Jesus asked his disciples who they thought he was, Peter replied for all, "Thou art the Christ, the Son of the living God!" When the centurion beside the cross saw Jesus die, he cried out, "Truly this man was the Son of God."

Among all the great of the world Jesus stands out in matchless superiority. History has no record of any other such man or any other such life. No one else ever left such an impress upon the ages. He was the Son of God, or He could not have been what He was. We can never be satisfied until we fall in worship before Him, and own Him as our living Lord.

O matchless Christ, I bow in loving worship before Thee and proclaim, "Of a truth Thou art the Son of God."

18

True Worship

Is it not to deal thy bread to the hungry, and that thou bring the poor that are cast out to thy house? when thou seest the naked, that thou cover him; and that thou hide not thyself from thine own flesh?

—Isa. 58:7

HIGH IN THE Sierra Nevada mountains of California are great reservoirs of blue water. They are lovely to look at, and pleasant to sail and fish. But their true purpose is realized only when their waters are channeled into pipes and brought down the mountainside to water the fields and provide drink for man and beast.

Formal worship of God is not enough. Isaiah says that if it consists only of fasting, of bowing down the head as a bulrush, of spreading sackcloth and ashes, it means nothing to Him.

The fast that God delights in, he says, is "to loose the bands of wickedness, to undo the heavy burdens, and to let the oppressed go free, and that ye break every yoke."

God will honor such worship. "Then shall thy light break forth as the morning, and thine health shall spring forth speedily; and thy righteousness shall go before thee: the glory of the Lord shall be thy rereward. Then shalt thou call, and the Lord shall answer; thou shalt cry, and he shall say, Here I am."

Teach me, O Lord, to worship Thee in spirit and in truth. Help me to make my worship real through Christian living.

Read Isa. 58:13-14

Our Father's House

And he came to Nazareth, where he had been brought up: and, as his custom was, he went into the synagogue on the sabbath day. —Luke 4:16

IN THE DAYS before the installation of hearing aids in churches, a certain woman with impaired hearing was seen to be in her seat at every service. Everyone knew that she did not hear any of the service. One day friends asked her why she came.

"This is my Father's house," she replied. "He expects me to be here."

The Sabbath is a sacred gift. It is set apart from the other days of the week. Only as we hallow its spirit and guard its occupations can we appropriate its blessings.

When church bells ring on the Sabbath, let us lay aside our busy plans and seek our Father's house. There the world falls off, cool waters quench our thirsty hearts, and living bread satisfies our hungry souls. A sense of the unseen world and its spiritual values revives within us.

"He expects me to be there." He offers me rest and gladness, tender memories, holy inspirations, and sweet fellowships. "I was glad when they said unto me, Let us go into the house of the Lord."

Father, I thank Thee for Thy house, and for the blessings which await me there.

We Need the Church

If we walk in the light, as he is in the light, we have fellow-
ship one with another. —*I John 1:7*

JON MORROW LINDBERGH, son of the famous "Lone Eagle," and two companions explored in 1951 the St. Elias Range in Alaska. Lashed together with long ropes, the three toiled up Mount Bear and came to a bridge of ice across a crevasse ninety feet deep. Al Baxter, in front, picked his way out on it. Suddenly the ice broke and he plunged through the hole. Jon was jerked from his feet but found enough traction in the deep snow to hold the saving rope while the third man, Bud Gates, threw Al a loop with which to climb back to solid ground.

The Christian Church offers us a fellowship which supports us throughout life. The sharing of God's love is a tie that binds our hearts together and keeps us from falling.

Attending church helps us to solve our problems, and gives us a new point of view. It helps to relieve us of our tensions. It brings us new strength to attack our loneliness and anxieties. It helps us to get through the difficult experiences of life.

Attending church helps us to gain an inner security. It enables us to face life and accept the results of our own decisions. It builds our character by making us aware that we are potentially children of God and precious in His sight. It helps us to become true sons of God.

Gracious God, I need the ministry of Thy holy Church. I will seek the fellowship of other Christians.

Fellowship

And they continued stedfastly in the apostles' doctrine and fellowship, and in breaking of bread, and in prayers.

—Acts 2:42

A MAN visiting a telescope factory stood watching a workman polish a lens with the palm of his hand.

"Why is it necessary to use your hand?" he asked.

"There comes a time in the making of a fine lens," replied the workman, "when nothing can be substituted for the human touch."

The early Christians shared their spiritual experiences with one another. They did everything in their power to keep God's love burning brightly in the heart of each member. They ate together, they prayed together, they sang together, and they exhorted one another in the Christian faith. They kept it alive by the human touch.

They were mindful of one another's welfare. What touched one touched them all. They shared their sorrows, dangers, duties, joys, their prosperity or adversity. They made provision for practical help for one another, giving as the Lord had prospered them for the relief of the poor saints, and distributing this money regularly to those in need.

When we share our experiences and gifts, we build one another up. We find our strength in bonds of fellowship.

Dear Lord, help me to love my fellow Christians and to be aware of their needs.

Our Promises

When thou vowest a vow unto God, defer not to pay it . . . :
pay that which thou hast vowed. —Eccl. 5:4

FRANCIS E. WILLARD wrote a biography of her sister Mary, entitled *Nineteen Beautiful Years*. She says that it was Mary's habit, as the girls were preparing for bed at night, to say, "Frank, let's read over our promises." She referred to the vows they took when they united with the church.

If this habit were adopted by church members over the world, it would change the life of the church and the world as well. One day in the past we made some promises which we intended to keep. But the years have passed, and just what the promises were we hardly remember. And so our own religious experience has been poorer, and the cause of Christ has suffered. It is easy to look up those vows. They concern such things as the keeping of God's holy will and commandments, the confession of Christ as Saviour, and loyalty to His Church. They are the means by which the soul grows in stature, and the Christian graces grow.

> Blessed Master, I have promised,
>   Hear my solemn vow;
> Take this pledge of mine and seal it
>   Here and now.
> —CHARLES A. DICKINSON

Blessed Master, help me to remember the vows I once made at Thine altar.

23

Read Luke 22:7-20

In Remembrance of Me

This do in remembrance of me.—Luke 22:19

IN OLDEN DAYS the early Christians partook of the Holy Communion in real and simple form. They knew nothing of the stately ritual, the organ music, the fair linen of later days. As they wandered over the familiar Galilean countryside where once they had walked with the Master, they paused and remembered Him. In grateful love they broke their bread and squeezed the grape.

In the celebration of the Holy Communion we take the cup of wine which is the symbol of the very life of Christ to our souls. As we partake of it and the bread, the springs of life itself within us are renewed. This is a privilege we can ill afford to miss when it is offered by our church. We should anticipate it eagerly. When Jesus instituted this act of remembrance for His followers, He said, "With desire I have desired to eat this passover with you before I suffer." He is longing to give us this new life.

At the Lord's table we unite in a great fellowship with His followers everywhere in time and in eternity. We remember Christians around the world. We draw near in thought and feeling to those who have entered into the heavenly life.

Grant me, gracious Lord, so to partake of the memorials of Thy Son Jesus Christ that I may be filled with the fullness of His life.

The Breaking of Bread

Christ our passover is sacrificed for us: therefore let us keep the feast.
                                                    —*I Cor. 5:7-8*

AN OLD LEGEND of the East tells us that when Zacchaeus was old he still lived in Jericho. Every morning he went to the tree from which he first saw the Lord. He poured water around its roots, pulled the weeds, and passed his hand lovingly over the trunk of the tree. He looked up at the place where he had sat that day when he first saw Jesus. Then with a smile of gratitude he turned homeward, calm and happy for the day's work. He explained it by saying, "It was that tree which brought me to Him whom my soul loveth."

Every true life has its sacred memory spots. These places should be kept green and fresh by grateful service.

The word "sacrament" comes from the Latin word *sacramentum*. It expresses the oath of the Roman soldier to Caesar. He declared that he was willing to go anywhere, to do anything, and to die if necessary for the emperor.

When we attend upon the service of the Sacrament of the Lord's Supper, it is a watering of the roots of the Christian life. It is a visit to the tree. It is a keeping of the places of spiritual blessing fresh and green. It is a renewal of our pledge of obedience and loyalty to our Master.

My gracious Lord, I love to remember Thy sacrifice for me. I renew my loyalty to Thee.

The Inevitable One

Abide in me, and I in you. As the branch cannot bear fruit of itself, except it abide in the vine; no more can ye, except ye abide in me.   *—John 15:4*

FRANCIS THOMPSON described in marvelous poetry the pursuit of the soul of man by "The Hound of Heaven." The foolish soul strives in vain to escape its savior. It flees night and day "down the arches of the years." It tries to hide "in the mist of tears" and "under running laughter." But ever it hears the sound of following Feet and a Voice. At last the chase is ended, and the Voice surrounds it "like a bursting sea," saying, "I am He whom thou seekest!"

In the evening of the day of resurrection the disciples were together in the upper room. They were perplexed, and frightened. They fastened the door shut. Yet suddenly Jesus stood among them. They did not know how He came; they only knew He was with them and all their sorrow was gone.

We can never shut Jesus out of our lives. We may close the door against Him, but He is there nevertheless. He meets us at every turn in life's road, in its joys and in its tragedies. Moments out of the past, moments of happiness or of sorrow, return to remind us of Jesus. Jesus is inevitable.

"Thou hast created us unto Thyself," said Augustine, "and our heart finds no rest until it rests in Thee."

Dear Master, the thought of Thee is like music to my heart. I rejoice in the sunny peace of Thy presence.

All Things Become New

Therefore if any man be in Christ, he is a new creature: old things are passed away; behold, all things are become new.
—II Cor. 5:17

JENNY LIND, the celebrated Swedish soprano, was a woman of deep piety. When she discovered her powers as a singer, it transformed her whole outlook on life. She said, "I got up that morning one creature; I went to bed another creature."

Each one of us, in a large measure, creates his own world. If we are despondent, we drape the world in black. If we are cheerful, we fill the world about us with sunshine. If we change ourselves, we change our world.

When we let Christ into our lives, we create a whole new world for ourselves. We become spiritually alive and move in an atmosphere of joy and power.

We have a new attitude toward Christ. He becomes the center of our life. His will is our chief desire. His love is our highest motive.

We have a new feeling toward our fellow men. We love them. We want to serve them.

We have a new attitude toward our own lives. We no longer seek comfort and pleasure for ourselves alone. We want to share Christ with all men everywhere.

My Father, make me a new creature in Christ. May His love be the great motive of my life.

27

All Glorious Within

The king's daughter is all glorious within.—Ps. 45:13

ONE EVENING as I walked along a quiet street in the twilight, the dark outline of a great church loomed ahead. Suddenly the tall Gothic windows poured forth a radiance of exquisite color. The light had been turned on within. What a moment before had been dull leaded glass was now a miracle of beauty.

Something like that happens in the human heart when Christ enters into it. All becomes glorious within. High and holy aspirations are born. Pure and lovely thoughts find a home. Kind and generous impulses crowd out all that is selfish and sinful. Joy and peace flood the soul.

The beauty of the Master shines out in the faces of His followers like the radiant colors of a church window. It speaks in gentleness and kindness. It shows in poise and calmness of behavior. It draws other people to its sources.

> God be in my head,
>   And in my understanding;
> God be in my eyes,
>   And in my looking;
> God be in my mouth,
>   And in my speaking;
> God be in my heart,
>   And in my thinking.

> —SARUM PRIMER

Lord, shine through me that I may point others to Thee.

Friends of the Master

And they took knowledge of them, that they had been with Jesus.   *—Acts 4:13*

A SIX-YEAR-OLD BOY recited the beatitude, "Blessed are the pure in heart: for they shall see God." His mother asked him if he knew what the verse meant.

"No," he replied, "but it makes me think of my Sunday-school teacher."

Companionship and friendship produce similarities in people. Those bound by great love often grow to look alike through the years. This carries over into the spiritual realm as well. The friends of the Master grow to be like Him. They remind others of Him by their gentleness, compassion, and goodness.

> Not merely in the words you say,
>   Not only in your deeds confessed,
> But in the most unconscious way
>   Is Christ expressed.
>
> .   .   .   .
>
> And from your eyes He beckons me,
>   And from your heart His love is shed,
> Till I lose sight of you—and see
>   The Christ instead.
>
>   —AUTHOR UNKNOWN

May I grow to be like Thee, Dear Master, and remind others of Thy loving ways.

Looking Unto Jesus

Looking unto Jesus the author and finisher of our faith.
—Heb. 12:2

Every morning lean thine arms awhile
Upon the window sill of heaven
And gaze upon thy Lord,
Then, with the vision in thy heart
Turn strong to meet thy day.

—AUTHOR UNKNOWN

A WOMAN who was confined to her bed asked that the light be turned out in her room very early in the evening. Knowing that she did not sleep until much later in the night, her friends expressed fear that she would be lonely.

"Oh no," she said. "When the light is out, I can think about my Lord. I am able to see His face more clearly."

As we grow in the Christian life, we find increasing joy in the contemplation of our blessed Lord. We see new beauty in Jesus' character as we dwell upon it. We find new meaning in the things He said and did as we daily study the records of them preserved for us in the Gospels. We grow in understanding of His spirit. And thus we grow in His likeness.

O God, my Father, I know that Thou art very near. I love to worship Thee as Thou hast shown Thyself in Thy Son Jesus Christ.

Lovers' Lane

The Lord is at hand.—Phil. 4:5

ON A CLIFF above the blue Pacific Ocean at one time there stretched an avenue of giant pine trees four deep. The path among them was soft with pine needles, and the air was sweet with their fragrance. The surf breaking on the rocks below was music to the ear. This avenue was known as "Lovers' Lane." Friends loved to walk there in the beauty of nature and of their own companionship.

Any walk may become a Lovers' Lane for us if we picture Christ beside us as we go about our daily tasks. Whatever else the words, "The Lord is at hand," may mean, they tell us that He is always ready to share our experiences.

> I almost never say my prayers
> With smoothly folded eyes—
> So many prayers go blundering
> Each day to paradise.
>
> .   .   .   .   .
>
> I wait until some cool, fresh dawn
> When He goes down our walk,
> And then I run and slip my hand
> Within His hand and talk.
>
> —ELLINOR L. NORCROSS

Jesus, Lover of my Soul, walk with me through this day, that I may rejoice in Thy companionship.

Read Matt. 9:20-22

Only Believe

Therefore I say unto you, What things soever ye desire, when ye pray, believe that ye receive them, and ye shall have them.
—Mark 11:24

E. STANLEY JONES tells of a Chinese gentleman in Penang who, sitting in his new automobile, had coolies push him up and down the street. He was asked if there wasn't any power in the machine.

"Yes," he replied, "but I am afraid to turn it on."

When the sick woman reached out her hand in the throng and touched the hem of Christ's garment, she was made whole. Her act of faith laid hold of the mighty power of God. She was not afraid to tap the source.

Many people pray because they have been taught to pray as children. Some pray because they want to believe that somewhere there is a power which they can reach in time of need. They hope their prayers will be answered, but they are not sure.

It is a far different thing to believe that there is One with the heart of a Father who listens for the voice of His child and who answers his cry. When a man believes that, he can put his faith into action. All of God's resources become available to him. He meets life triumphantly.

Eternal source of all power, give me the will to act upon my beliefs today. Flood my life with Thy power.

Constant in Prayer

In the morning, rising up a great while before day, he . . . departed into a solitary place, and there prayed.—Mark 1:35

ANTON RUBINSTEIN, famous Russian pianist of the last century, said, "If I omit practice one day, I notice it; if I omit it for two days, my friends notice it; if I omit it for three days, the public notices it."

Schools have schedules for classes, railroads have timetables for trains, and factories have hours and shifts for their workmen. Schedules are important. Life would be a hopeless tangle if they were not set up and followed.

This pertains also to our prayer life. If we are not regular in prayer, we notice it first in our feelings toward God. If we neglect it too long, our friends notice it in our relationship with them.

Prayer should become a habit. We will then turn to it as naturally as we turn to food for our bodies. When it becomes a habit, we do not have to debate the question every day. We give it first place and arrange other engagements around it. It becomes a sacred time.

We hurry to the presence of the person we love most dearly. We pour out our love without reserve. So shall we seek our Father's presence. He is waiting there to bless us.

O God, give me a new desire for prayer. May I depend upon it as I depend upon my daily food.

The Quiet Time

Evening, and morning, and at noon, will I pray.—Ps. 55:17

LYNN J. RADCLIFFE tells of a young associate of his, a missionary on furlough, who realized suddenly that he was neglecting to pray because of his crowded schedule of study and pastoral duties. He promised God that henceforth he would begin each day with prayer. That very night he studied late and woke next morning in time only for a quick breakfast before class. As he sat down at the table he remembered his promise. He returned to his room to pray and went to school hungry. Telling it later he added, "You know, the next morning I got up in time for breakfast, too!"

A definite time is necessary for daily prayer. If left to the circumstance of the day, it is likely to be neglected or forgotten. In the freshness of the dawn it is natural to turn to God in praise, and to seek guidance for the day. A withdrawal at the noon hour from the busy confusion of the world strengthens the spirit. When day is done, the heart turns to God for rest and contemplation. We may choose one of these periods, or better still all of them, for a daily habit.

An accustomed place for prayer lends itself to the habit of prayer. Familiar surroundings bring to remembrance our past experiences of prayer, and we more easily enter into its atmosphere.

"Speak, Lord, for Thy servant heareth."

The Closed Door

But thou, when thou prayest, enter into thy closet, and when thou hast shut thy door, pray to thy Father which is in secret; and thy Father which seeth in secret shall reward thee openly.
                                                    —*Matt. 6:6*

A MAN went into a telephone booth to make a call. He got his friend on the wire, but had great difficulty in hearing him. "Speak louder," he shouted into the receiver.

Finally his friend succeeded in saying to him, "If you will close the door of your telephone booth, you will be able to hear what I am saying to you."

In prayer we often do not establish any connection between God and ourselves because we fail to shut the door upon the noise and confusion of life. It is necessary to shut the door against the ringing of the telephone, the conversation of the family, the playing of the radio and television. We must banish the noises within our hearts also—the problems, the hurts, the cares.

In silent awe and adoration we wait before Him. We feel His presence near. Then we are ready to speak aloud our thanksgiving and supplications.

Speak to Him, thou, for He hears, and Spirit with Spirit can meet—
Closer is He than breathing, and nearer than hands and feet.
                                                    —ALFRED TENNYSON

I will seek Thee in silence, my Father, that I may hear Thy voice.

Spiritual Fragrance

*Now thanks be unto God, which always causeth us to triumph
in Christ, and maketh manifest the savour of his knowledge by
us in every place.* —II Cor. 2:14

FOR THE WORD "savour" the new Revised Standard Version
substitutes the more familiar word "fragrance," making the
verse read: "God . . . through us spreads the fragrance of the
knowledge of him everywhere."

In the high-class Christian homes of India there is a small
room set apart for devotion. Every morning the young Indian
girl bathes and dresses in fresh garments. Then she goes to this
quiet room and offers her morning worship of prayer and
thanksgiving to God. Before she leaves the room, she takes a
flask of perfume and bathes her feet with it. Slipping on her
sandals, she goes out to her household duties and pleasures.
She carries the fragrance of her prayer hour with her, and is
reminded of God throughout the day.

We may not anoint our hands or feet with perfume as we
leave our morning devotions. But we may carry a fragrance
with us that other people will recognize. We may carry also
a sense of victory as we meet the problems of the day.

In the Revelation John speaks of the prayers of the saints as
sweet odors in golden vials before the throne of God. The sweet
odor of prayer delights the heart of God as well as man.

*My Father, may those around me today be aware of my
friendship with the Master.*

36

Wait

*The Lord is good unto them that wait for him, to the soul
that seeketh him.* 　　　　　　　　　　　　　*—Lam. 3:25*

HAVE YOU ever waited for the return of someone dear to you?
You find yourself turning again and again to the window
hoping to catch the first sight of the familiar form. It may grow
late. You go to the door and peer out into the darkness. But you
have no doubt about his coming. He told you he would come.
You have only to watch and wait.

There is a word in the book of Psalms that is often repeated.
It is the word "wait." For example: "Wait on the Lord: be of
good courage, and he will strengthen thine heart: wait, I say,
on the Lord." The word suggests a confident expectation, a
sure belief that He will hear and will answer. It means a hold-
ing on.

An important part of communion with God is the waiting
time. After we have expressed our thanksgiving and voiced
our petitions, we need to wait before Him. We need to grow
still and listen for His answer to our prayer. It will come in a
feeling of new strength. Often it comes in a clear realization of
direction for the path ahead. It will always bring a sense of
His presence.

*Forbid, O Lord, that I should hurry out of Thy presence
without waiting for Thine answer. Teach me to wait before
Thee.*

Prayer Jewels

Men ought always to pray and not to faint.—Luke 18:1

A KING and his horsemen traveled one day through an enchanted cavern. Sparkling gems lay beneath the horses' feet, lighting the way through the darkness.

"He who picks up these stones will be sorry," a mysterious voice cried out to them. "But he who picks up none will be more sorry."

Some of the men picked up a few of the stones, but others feared to take them and gathered none. As they emerged from the cavern, the mouth of it closed behind them. Those who had picked up a few of the gems were sorry they had not picked up more; those who had picked up none were still more sorry, for the stones were of fabulous value.

Our prayer time is like this legend. At the end of the day we will be glad if we have gathered the jewels of prayer. If we have neglected to pray, we can never go back and recapture the blessings we have missed. Our days will be rich in proportion to the time we spend in communion with God.

Someone has said: "He who saves his time from prayer shall lose it; but he who loses his time for prayer and communion with God will find it again with added power and blessing."

My Father, teach me how to pray. Give me assurance that Thou art always near and hearest my voice.

Answer to Prayer

The Lord is nigh unto all them that call upon him, to all that call upon him in truth.   —*Ps. 145:18*

THE AIR about us is filled with so many radio waves that if we were able to hear them all we would be overcome. However, we may, by tuning a radio to a certain wave length, catch the one message we want.

Our human minds are inadequate for the full comprehension of God's greatness and power. But by the simple exercise of faith we may reach out to Him and feel His loving response.

> If radio's slim fingers
>   Can pluck a melody
> From night, and toss it over
>   A continent, or sea;
>
> If the petalled white notes
>   Of a violin
> Are blown across a mountain,
>   Or a city's din;
>
> If songs, like crimson roses,
>   Are culled from thin blue air,
> Why should mortals wonder
>   If God hears prayer?
>   —ETHEL ROMIG FULLER

O God, tune my spirit to Thine that I may hear Thy voice speaking to me.

Read Luke 11:5-13

Unanswered Prayer

*And I say unto you, Ask, and it shall be given you; seek, and
ye shall find; knock, and it shall be opened unto you.*
—Luke 11:9

THERE IS a paradox of prayer. The prayer that seems to go unanswered may in reality be the one God answers in the truest
sense. We ask as little children ask, not knowing our real need.
We fail to see beyond the present moment. God in His infinite wisdom desires our highest good and answers our hearts'
yearnings in better ways than we ask.

> He prayed for strength that he might achieve;
> He was made weak that he might obey.
> He prayed for wealth that he might do greater things;
> He was given infirmity that he might do better things.
> He prayed for riches that he might be happy;
> He was given poverty that he might be wise.
> He prayed for power that he might have the praise of men;
> He was given infirmity that he might feel the need of God.
> He prayed for all things that he might enjoy life;
> He was given life that he might enjoy all things.
> He had received nothing that he asked for—all that he hoped for;
> His prayer was answered—he was most blessed.
>
> —AUTHOR UNKNOWN

*My Father, when my prayers seem to be unanswered, help
me to know that Thou hast some better thing in store for me.*

Loving Your Neighbor on Your Knees

I pray for them.—John 17:9

"INTERCESSORY PRAYER," said Charles Brent, "might be defined as loving your neighbor on your knees."

Praying for others makes a difference in your feeling for the ones you pray for. You come to love them. They also begin to feel different toward you.

All men pray for those they love. Intercessory prayer is the most earnest prayer of all. It puts the good of others above your own. You identify yourself with God that His will may be done in other lives.

Jesus spent most of his prayer time praying for others, not for himself. He said to Peter, "I have prayed for thee." He prayed in the upper room, "Neither pray I for these alone, but for them also which shall believe on me through their word." He is still praying for his followers, "He ever liveth to make intercession for them."

> The weary one had rest, the sad had joy
>   That day, and wondered how?
> A ploughman singing at his work had prayed,
>   "Lord, help them now."
>
> —AUTHOR UNKNOWN

Into Thy loving care, O Father, I place those who are dearest to me. Do for them the things I cannot do.

Read Rom. 15:25-33

Your Part

Now I beseech you, brethren, for the Lord Jesus Christ's sake, and for the love of the Spirit, that ye strive together with me in your prayers to God for me. —Rom. 15:30

MRS. WALTER R. LAMBUTH, wife of the great missionary bishop, was an invalid for many years and could not travel with her husband. She told how for many months she had been praying for the Korean people.

"Little did I realize," she said, "how God would use me to answer my own prayer by calling my husband to go to Korea to serve these people."

God expects us to co-operate with Him when we pray. We must help to answer our own prayers. He does not do for us the things we can do ourselves. If we pray for health, we must obey the laws of health. If we pray for the poor, we must make our own gift for their relief. If we pray for the peace of the world, we must first have peace within our own hearts and in our dealings with our fellow men. Otherwise our prayers are futile and only wishful thinking. A great Christian has said, "It is not possible for us to live one way and to pray another."

Said one little girl to another, "I am afraid we are going to be late to school. Let's stop and pray about it."

"No," was the reply. "Let's pray as we run."

Make me willing, O God, to work with Thee to answer my own prayers.

Ecstasy

And after six days Jesus taketh Peter, James, and John his brother, and bringeth them up into an high mountain apart, and was transfigured before them. . . . Then answered Peter, and said unto Jesus, Lord, it is good for us to be here.

—Matt. 17:1-2, 4

IN A POEM by Charles T. Brooks, an aged monk kneels upon the pavement of his cell and prays that he may be given a vision of the Lord Christ. As he bows in prayer a wondrous light fills the room. He beholds before him the glorious form of the Master. Then upon the stillness breaks the tones of the bell at the monastery gate. The poor and hungry wait to be fed. Wistfully from his knees he rises and goes upon his act of mercy. When he returns at last, he finds the vision more radiant and hears the words, "Hadst thou stayed, I must have fled."

Jesus' faithful three beheld his glory upon the mount and prayed to remain forever in its light. But the Master led them down the mountain to a place where a little boy waited to be cured of his sickness.

Moments of ecstasy of prayer are given to call us to greater devotion. Our moments of rapture must find expression in loving service for the Master, or we shall lose them. When we do good in His name and care for the least of these, He will be near. He will receive the deed as done unto Him.

O Lord, I thank Thee for the moments when Thou art very near. Use me then in some humble way to bless another.

In the Mind of God

The Lord thinketh upon me: thou art my help and my de-liverer; make no tarrying, O my God.   —*Ps. 40:17*

THE FATHER of Charlotte Brontë was an English minister. He was very careful of the education of his three little girls, all of whom in later life became well-known novelists. It was his habit every morning at the breakfast table to ask a thought-provoking question of each one.

"What is there in the world today that was not there yesterday?" he said to Charlotte one morning.

"The primrose by the waterfall."

"And where was it yesterday?" he asked.

"In the mind of God."

God loves each one of His children in a unique way. He thinks about you just as you are. He knows where you are, how you live, and what you need. He has something in His mind for you each day. He sees the perfect person you may become by His help.

A little boy who lived in a temple once heard God's voice calling to him in the nighttime. He answered, "Speak; for thy servant heareth." God told him some of His secrets. Each day God wants to speak to you. If you answer as Samuel did, He will tell you what He has in mind for you.

Grant me grace, O Father, to discover each day Thy will for me, and obedience to walk in it.

"The Game with Minutes"

Pray without ceasing.—I Thess. 5:17

FRANK LAUBACH is one of the great missionaries of the world. He has written a little booklet called *The Game with Minutes and How to Play It*. He makes a game all day long of seeing how many minutes of the day he can bring God into his daily occupations. He talks to Him as he would to his earthly father, about all the happenings of the day. While he is walking or eating or speaking with someone, he finds moments to talk to God. He says it brings joy into each hour of the day, and helps to solve all of its problems.

Frank Laubach lives in the constant atmosphere of prayer. He believes there are hundreds of little bits of wasted time which may be filled with prayers ten seconds long. He says that when he thinks of people or meets them, he throws a cloak of prayer around them.

Our day may be enriched by this habit. When we glimpse a bit of beauty in the world, or catch a strain of melody, we may offer our thanksgiving. The sudden need of a neighbor may give the occasion to send a petition to the Source of help. Thus we may relate all of the day's happenings to God.

It takes practice to live like this. It takes unfailing love and unselfishness. It means the shifting of the center of life from self to God. It makes Christ real. It brings happiness.

My Father, I thank Thee for the joy of Thy daily companionship. I thank Thee that I may bring Thee into every hour.

Become a Pray-er

*And pray one for another. . . . The effectual fervent prayer
of a righteous man availeth much.*   —*Jas. 5:16*

"I HAVE FINISHED my lifework and have retired. There isn't
much left for me to do," said a certain person. That may be true
when applied to a commercial job, but it has no application
to the life of a Christian. A Christian never retires from God's
work. There is always work for him to do. The service one is
able to render in his mature years is usually the best service
of his life.

One of the most precious things in the world is time. Many
people have very little free time in the earlier years of life.
In later life they find that they have more of this valuable
commodity at their disposal. Active duties do not make the
same demands upon them. When we reach this period, we
may rejoice that we have the opportunity to serve God more
fully than ever before. We have the time to become a pray-er
for Him.

The world is full of prejudice and misunderstanding.
These evils can be banished only when they are replaced by
love. When enough people learn to love as Jesus loved, His
Kingdom will come. We now have the opportunity to help
bring this about. We can hold the world up to God in believing
prayer. Our time is needed for this great work.

*Use me, O Father, to serve the world by being a pray-er.
Help me to dedicate myself to this task.*

Mustard Seed Faith

If ye have faith as a grain of mustard seed, . . . nothing shall be impossible unto you. —Matt. 17:20

A SMALL GIFT BOX contained a gold chain from which hung a transparent ball. A genuine mustard seed was inside the little ball. A gift card bore the above scripture and the words, "This is your Mustard Seed Remembrancer. May it remind you frequently of this scripture. Keep it with you—and remember to have faith always."

A Remembrancer in ancient times was an officer in the Court of the Exchequer whose duty it was to remind officials of important events.

Thousands of people carry this little Mustard Seed Remembrancer to remind them that faith in God is the key for solving life's problems.

When God seems far away and we are fearful, it is usually our lack of faith. Confidence comes when we put problems into God's hands. We may begin with a very little faith, not bigger than the mustard seed, and then pray, "Lord, increase my faith." It will grow as the mustard grows until it is a great tree. And when there is great faith, there are miracles!

My Father, my faith in Thee is my dearest treasure. Help it to grow.

Hidden Treasure

The Spirit and the bride say, Come. And let him that heareth say, Come. And let him that is athirst come. And whosoever will, let him take the water of life freely.   —Rev. 22:17

IN *The Arabian Nights* there is a fantastic story about a remarkable ointment. If it is rubbed on the eyes, it will enable one to see all the riches in the world—the gold hidden in the mines and the diamonds treasured in the secret places.

The Bible is no imaginary ointment, but it is genuinely effectual to those who seek God. It enables us to see all the beauties and riches of God's world and unlocks for us the storehouse of His treasures for us.

The treasures of God's Word become ours when we appropriate their truths and make them a part of our daily lives. We discover these treasures by reading the Bible. They become our own when we study their meaning, and memorize their glorious passages. God is able then to recall to our minds the truths we need in special times of need. He guides and comforts us in this way.

How much of God's Word belongs to you? How many of His loving promises have you stored in your memory?

My Father, I thank Thee for the peace that comes to my heart through the promises which I find in Thy Word.

Stored Treasure

*Search the scriptures; for in them ye think ye have eternal
life: and they are they which testify of me.   —John 5:39*

BAGGAGE TAKEN ABOARD an ocean liner is carefully classified
and tagged. The pieces of luggage which will be used during
the crossing are placed in the passengers' staterooms. The
pieces which will not be needed until the voyage is over are
stored deep in the hold of the vessel. When the ship docks,
they are brought out and returned to their owners.

This is the manner in which some of us treat God's Word.
We carry it along with us, but we store it away in a safe place
and then forget about it. We pick up instead the morning paper
or the new magazine.

God's Word is the wisdom of the ages, the very nectar of
life. It is the depository of all the answers to our questions, of
all that we need for guidance, comfort, and courage.

As we grow older, His Word should become increasingly
dear to us. We have more time to read its pages and learn its
lessons. We are better able to understand its wisdom. We need
its comfort more.

"Thy word is a lamp unto my feet," said one who had found
the way to wisdom, "and a light unto my path."

*Open my eyes, O Lord, that I may find wondrous things in
Thy law. Help me to hide it in my heart.*

Quail or Gophers

Thy testimonies have I taken as an heritage for ever: for they are the rejoicing of my heart. I have inclined my heart to perform thy statutes alway, even unto the end.—Ps.119:111-12

A HUNTER took a new dog with him into the fields in search of quail. For some time the dog flushed the covies from the brush. But a rabbit crossed his path, and he was off after it. Then a squirrel appeared, and the dog gave chase. The last the hunter saw of him he was barking down a gopher hole.

Men find what they are looking for in God's Word. Some men read the Bible in search of history, and they discover the records of ancient tribes and civilizations. Some come to study the jurisprudence of early peoples. They find a decalogue that remains until this day the foundation of the moral code of the civilized world. Some come to delight in the beauty of its literature, and they discover drama and poetry which have never been surpassed.

Some men come to the Bible with hunger in their hearts for an understanding of God and His will in their lives. And they find what they are looking for.

I thank Thee, Lord, that in Thy Word are the answers to all my questions. Inspire me to search more diligently for the wisdom in its pages.

Memory Verses

Therefore shall ye lay up these words in your heart and in your soul, and bind them for a sign upon your hand, that they may be as frontlets between your eyes.   —Deut. 11:18

ISABELLA THOBURN, the first woman missionary appointed by The Methodist Church to go to India, walked home one evening from prayer meeting with a young preacher. Turning to him, she said, "Did you ever notice that many of our answers to prayer come to us through verses of Scripture we have memorized?"

God's Word in our mind is an endless source of guidance and comfort in the hard experiences of life.

God's Word in our heart saves us from moodiness and ill temper. It lets the sunlight in.

God's Word stored within us gives us a sense of His constant presence. We are continually reminded of Him.

A hospital experience becomes less difficult when one remembers the words, "Be merciful unto me, O God, . . . for my soul trusteth in thee: yea, in the shadow of thy wings will I make my refuge, until these calamities be overpast."

When loved ones slip away, we find a strong anchor if within our hearts we hear the words, "Yea, though I walk through the valley of the shadow of death, I will fear no evil: for thou art with me; thy rod and thy staff they comfort me."

May Thy words speak within my heart each day, O God.

Taking Blessings for Granted

Moreover Job continued his parable, and said, Oh that I were
as in months past, as in the days when God preserved me.
—Job 29:1-2

TODAY IN AMERICA our highways are streaming with fast cars,
the streets are crowded with hurrying people, and the beaches
are thronged with young and old who are searching for pleasure. Everywhere people are seeking something new to satisfy
the restlessness within their hearts.

Job was the greatest man of all the East. He possessed wealth
and honor, a home and family, and every blessing the heart
could wish. Did he take these blessings for granted when he
had them? Most of us do. Did he sometimes think his days
were humdrum and uninteresting? Most of us complain of
that. After these blessings were gone and he looked back upon
them, how rich they seemed!

We do not have to go outside our homes to find happiness.
The truest joys lie at our own doorstep and within our own
hearts. If we search, we will find them in loved ones, home,
health, and homely duties. When we take these blessings for
granted, we miss their truest meaning.

Gracious Lord, help me to appreciate the blessings that are
mine today. Let me never take them for granted.

Pay in Kind

Be ye doers of the word, and not hearers only.—Jas. 1:22

ANNE LINDBERGH, in her book *Listen the Wind,* says, "One can never pay in gratitude; one can only pay 'in kind' somewhere else in life."

You have heard someone say, "That is one debt of gratitude I can never repay." That is always true when we think of what God has given us. It is often true of what others have given us. Jesus solves our problem in His words, "Inasmuch as ye have done it unto one of the least of these . . . , ye have done it unto me." When we pass along the blessing we have received to someone else, we pay our debt of gratitude to the one who gave it to us.

This does not relieve us of expressing our appreciation in words. But words are not enough. We must pay "in kind."

> Have you had a kindness shown?
>   Pass it on.
> It was not given to you alone,
>   Pass it on.
> Let it travel through the years;
> Let it wipe another's tears;
> Till in heaven the deed appears,
>   Pass it on.

—HENRY BURTON

I am a debtor, O Lord, to Thee and to my fellow men. Help me to pay this debt by loving service for others.

A Debt

For unto whomsoever much is given, of him shall be much required. —Luke 12:48

ALBERT SCHWEITZER is one of the great servants of mankind. He turned aside from triumphs in music, philosophy, literature, and theology, and prepared himself to go as a healer of sick bodies and souls in French Equatorial Africa. He took literally the words of Jesus, "Heal the sick, . . . cast out devils: freely ye have received, freely give. "

His dedication grew out of his compassion for the sufferings of the world, and his gratitude for his own advantages in life. He felt that he had no right to take for granted his happy youth, his good health, and his abilities.

He says, "We must not treat ourselves as being for ourselves alone. Whoever is spared personal pain must feel himself called to diminish the pain of others."

Most of us are particular about financial obligations. On the first day of the month we settle our accounts and protect our honor. There are other debts which we often forget. When we awake in the morning to sunshine and bird song, and to the comforts of home, we are in debt. When we retain our health, we are in debt. When we cherish friends and loved ones, we are in debt. We may pay only by being kind to some other of God's children.

I pray that I may be ever mindful of my debt to Thee, O God. Show me how to repay by serving others.

Offer Praise to God

I will praise thee, O Lord, with my whole heart.—Ps. 9:1

A YOUNG WOMAN walking by a church on a weekday saw a little girl coming out.

"Where have you been, my dear?" she asked.

"In there."

"And what were you doing there?"

"Just praying."

Thinking perhaps that the child was troubled about something, she inquired, "And what did you ask God for?"

"Oh, nothing. I was just loving God a little."

Someone has pointed out how strange it is that most of us never think to do for God what we habitually do for our human loved ones. We try to be happy at the breakfast table. We send them forth to meet the work of the day with words of cheer. We try not to add to their burden by our own moods of gloom and anxiety.

How often we fail to do the same for God! We tell Him only our needs and troubles. We pour out our sorrows. Does He not love our joyousness, our words of love? He looks down upon His warring world. He hears the cries of His suffering children. His burdens are beyond our thought. Who can say that His burdens would not be lighter if we offered to Him our gladness each day? Why not begin today?

O God, my Father, I love to worship Thee. Wilt Thou accept the offering of my love and peace that I bring Thee this day?

A Cloud of Witnesses

Wherefore seeing we also are compassed about with so great a cloud of witnesses. . . .
—*Heb. 12:1*

AMONG THE PORTRAITS painted by the artist Avery Handly is one of Robert E. Lee. The artist saw service in World War II. Later he said, "While on duty in the Navy, I found myself often staring into the Jovian face of Lee and receiving courage from it."

We receive strength when we remember great souls we have known. We see the nobility of their lives more clearly through the perspective of years. We see the finished life as it is related to God and its fellow men. They are faint pictures of One who is better than all of them, and in whose image they were made.

The face of a great teacher, the remembrance of a loved pastor, the voice of a noble friend, call to us from the past. They stir our flagging spirits and comfort our yearning hearts. Our cloud of witnesses is ever around us to bless. As we open our minds and hearts to them, they catch us up in loving embrace and draw us closer to God. We rise through them to the perfect One, whose beauty is ever wooing us to better living.

My Father, I am grateful for these men and women I have known whose lives have touched my own for good.

Golden Memories

*I have considered the days of old. . . . I call to remembrance
my song in the night.*
—Ps. 77:5-6

A CROCHETED BEDSPREAD can be full of golden memories. Experiences of the past are woven into all its threads: afternoons on sunlit porches, evenings in fire-lighted rooms, hours spent with dear ones. In remembrance we see little children playing at our knees; we hear the voices of friends of yesteryear. Today we draw these memories like a fairy mantle around our hearts to warm and comfort us.

Memories are one of God's ways of teaching us wisdom. We build upon the experiences of the past. We see our mistakes in truer light. We learn lessons and grow in knowledge.

Memories are also one of His provisions for present joys. Our hearts are cheered when we recall the happiness of past days. We rejoice when we remember the good and great lives which have touched ours in other years.

When we dream of the past, let us dwell upon the golden memories which bless our lives. Let us forget the sad and unpleasant ones. They can no longer hurt us if we refuse to hold them in our hearts.

Dear Father, I thank Thee for all the golden memories of days gone by. Let me use the experiences of the past to enrich my life and the lives of others.

Think on Beautiful Things

Finally, brethren, whatsoever things are true, whatsoever thing are honest, whatsoever things are just, whatsoever things are pure, whatsoever things are lovely, whatsoever things are of good report; if there be any virtue, and if there be any praise, think on these things.   *—Phil. 4:8*

BALZAC, THE GREAT French novelist, lived in a garret during his early life. The room was nearly bare of furnishings. The fireplace was always cold and empty. But it is said that on the wall on one side of the room was written, "Painting by Leonardo da Vinci." On the opposite wall was written, "Gobelin Tapestry." And in the place of honor over the mantle was written, "Madonna by Raphael."

Despite his poverty Balzac lived in a world of beauty. He kept within his mind pictures of lovely things. In his imagination he lived in a room filled with the world's finest art.

Our surroundings may not always be what we would like. We cannot always choose where we live or what we live with. But we can furnish our inner lives with beauty. We can think upon great literature, fine works of art, sublime scenes of nature, and noble men and women. We can meditate upon the goodness of God. "For as he thinketh in his heart, so is he."

My Father, I open the windows of my heart to Thee that the radiance of Thy presence may fill every part of it.

The Beauty of the World

The earth is the Lord's, and the fullness thereof; the world,
and they that dwell therein. —Ps. 24:1

GOOD HOUSEWIVES know that it is necessary periodically to carry woolen bedclothes and garments out into the sunshine, and to spread them upon clotheslines so that the sun and wind may cleanse them and make them sweet again.

It is strange that we take so much better care of our material possessions than we do of our souls. We let trivial things prevent us from going out each day into God's beautiful out-of-doors. The rosy dawn, the sunset's splendor, the moon-silvered lake, the white bloom of an orchard, the glow of red roses, are wings upon which we fly to God in adoration. Our physical bodies are cleansed, and our hearts forget their broodings when we rejoice in the beauty around us. Often it takes some duty which must be performed regularly to call us forth. A little garden plot is a good incentive.

Rebecca McCann's "Cheerful Cherub," who charmed us with his quaint wisdom a few years ago, says:

> I went out to a well one night,
>   Soft darkness hid all day-time scars.
> I held some water to the light
>   And drank a dipper full of stars.

Father, I thank Thee for revealing Thyself to me in the
beauty of Thy world. May I drink deeply at this fountain.

A Watered Garden

And thou shalt be like a watered garden, and like a spring of water, whose waters fail not.   —Isa. 58:11

HELEN KELLER loves her garden. Of it she wrote:

> I run with playful winds that blow the scent
> Of rose and jessamine in eddying whirls.
> At last I come where tall lilies grow,
> Lifting their faces like white saints to God.
> While the lilies pray, I kneel upon the ground;
> I have strayed into the holy temple of the Lord.

We rejoice in the radiant life of a watered garden. Beauty is there: flowers bloom, perfume scents the air, birds sing, trees cast their cooling shade. There is glory in a garden.

But there is also work to be done in a garden. Much time must be spent upon your knees. There are sand and loam to sift, seeds to plant, weeds to pull. You must earn the beauty that is to follow.

Your life will blossom into beauty only if you earn it. You must get down on your knees. You must work. You must cooperate with God's laws. You must be patient. You must be humble.

Make my heart, O Father, like a watered garden, full of life and beauty.

Exceeding Glory

For our light affliction, which is but for a moment, worketh for us a far more exceeding and eternal weight of glory.
—II Cor. 4:17

AT THE GRADUATION EXERCISES of a great university one student received all the highest awards. When his name was called to receive his honors, he was led to the platform by a fellow student. He was blind. He had mastered his lessons by hearing them read to him by his fellow students.

When defeat stares a person in the face, it does one of two things to him. It calls forth supernatural abilities in him and drives him to superior accomplishment. Or it robs him of endeavor and kills his spirit. Everything depends on the man himself. He may take it either way.

> Defeat may serve as well as victory
> To shake the soul and let the glory out.
> When the great oak is straining in the wind,
> The boughs drink in new beauty, and the trunk
> Sends down a deeper root on the windward side.
> Only the soul that knows the mighty grief
> Can know the mighty rapture. Sorrows come
> To stretch our spaces in the heart of joy.
>
> —EDWIN MARKHAM

Strong Son of God, give me courage to change my defeats into victories.

Make the Most of It

*Why art thou cast down, O my soul? And why art thou dis-
quieted within me? hope in God.* —Ps. 43:5

THE ACTRESS MARGARET HAMILTON has played "battle-ax" roles
in seventy-five movies because she is so homely. She says,
"I'm glad I'm homely. My face has given me lots of work. I
remember the 'Wizard of Oz' set. They put a sign on my chair:
'Mag the Hag.' My, I just loved it. I'm not sensitive about my
looks. I've got what God gave me, and I make the most of it.
Happiness has nothing to do with what you look like. Accept
what you have and enjoy it. It's what's on the inside of you
that counts."

Most people do not happen to have looks that set them apart
in the minds of others, but many with far less cause fall into
the habit of self-pity. They persist in making themselves miser-
able.

Disappointments and frustrations are common to most men.
The test is how you meet them. When you fall into self-pity, all
of your interests and energies turn inward and poison your
heart. It is better to say, "Yes, I'm homely. I've had misfortune.
I've lost my loved one. I've been hurt by a friend. But I'll rise
above it. I'll turn it into something good with which to make
others happy."

*Dear Lord, deliver me from the sin of self-pity. Help me to
turn my losses into others' gains.*

Shining Courage

Be strong and of a good courage; be not afraid, neither be thou dismayed: for the Lord thy God is with thee whithersoever thou goest.

—Josh. 1:9

SUSAN PETERS was on the way to movie stardom when a hunting accident paralyzed her from the waist down. Soon afterward she went to a veteran's hospital to entertain the patients. When her car drew to the curb, a crowd of veterans was gathered. An orderly pushed up a wheel chair.

"You may lift me into the chair," she said.

He shook his head. "We get into our own chairs here."

She hesitated, fearing to fail before so many eyes. Then, making a supreme effort, she gave a leap and landed safely. Loud applause arose from the crowd. Her little act of courage cheered them more than any entertainment she could give.

The shining courage that sets one apart from his fellows costs a dear price. It is not something to inherit, or to gain by wistful longing. One must win it by victories within his heart. It springs from unfaltering faith, steadfast hope, and love undimmed by anything that may happen. It grows in daily prayer—a reinforcement for the soul wholly open and dedicated to God.

Dear Lord, may I so enter into Thy life that I may win courage. Help me to overcome any fear of physical harm, any shrinking from criticism, any dread of the future. I would face life bravely in Thy strength.

Read Eph. 6:1-10

Take the First Step

Finally, brethren, be strong in the Lord, and in the power of his might. —*Eph. 6:10*

THEODORE ROOSEVELT left behind him one of the finest examples of courage the world has seen. It was both physical and spiritual. It lasted throughout life. He overcame the handicap of a weak body in his youth. In old age he still faced life courageously.

At Oyster Bay, where he had retired to live, he developed sciatica and then inflammatory rheumatism. His doctors told him he might be forced to spend the rest of his life in a wheel chair. "All right," he answered after a pause, "I can live that way too!"

Courage consists of taking the first step. A swimmer hesitates on the seashore. He puts one foot in the water, and shivers all over. He takes another step, and a wave knocks him down. Finally he makes it out beyond the breakers where the water is deep and the swimming is grand.

New experiences, new places, new faces appear formidable, until we take the first step to meet them. They soon become as familiar and as comfortable as the old.

Amelia Earhart, first woman to fly the Atlantic, said: "Courage is the price that life exacts for granting peace."

Give me courage, O God, to face life with the strength Thou dost supply. Encourage me to take the first step into each new challenge life brings to me.

Just One Day at a Time

As thy days, so shall thy strength be.—Deut. 33:25

A WOMAN met with a serious accident. Surgery was necessary, followed by months in bed. When the physician had finished his work and was leaving, she asked him, "Doctor, how long will I have to lie here helpless in bed?"

"Oh," was the cheery reply, "just one day at a time."

Through the days that followed she found courage in the thought that she need bear her burden but one day at a time.

A task which lies ahead may seem impossible to accomplish. A burden may seem too great to bear. But when we break it up into small bits, the going becomes easy. The mastery of a textbook can never be accomplished as a whole. But when we take it chapter by chapter, day by day, we bring it about.

In the deeper realms of living, God offers us the same release. "As thy days, so shall thy strength be." Anyone can carry the burden of one day, or resist the temptation of one day. We pray for our daily bread, not for food of a lifetime. We need not count the years that lie ahead of us without the presence of a loved one. God asks only that we be brave one day at a time.

> Lord, for tomorrow and its needs
>   I do not pray;
> Keep me, my God, from stain of sin
>   Just for today.

—SYBIL F. PARTRIDGE

Merciful Father, give me strength just for today.

Use What You Have

For if there be first a willing mind, it is accepted according to that a man hath, and not according to that he hath not.
—II Cor. 8:12

IN FOREST LAWN MEMORIAL PARK in Glendale, California, stands a replica of Michelangelo's heroic statue of David with stone and sling in hand. Made of white Carrara marble, its majestic beauty stands in relief against the dark green of trees. It is said that Michelangelo was told he could not carve a statue of true proportions from a shaft of marble as narrow as the one at his disposal. His sublime art produced a perfect figure out of the material at hand.

Only a very few men or women live and work under perfect conditions. Nearly all work with limited means or under handicaps of some kind. No one by middle life has perfect health or boundless energy.

We must accept circumstances which cannot be changed, and start from where we find ourselves. We must use the materials we have at hand. They may seem inadequate for our task. It all depends on how we use them. A woman once said, "Anyone may be a good cook if she has unlimited choice of materials to work with. The real test is to be able to prepare an appetizing meal out of leftovers."

Dear Lord, I give the best that I have to Thee. Multiply it and use it for Thy glory.

Help Yourself

But let every man prove his own work, and then shall he have rejoicing in himself alone, and not in another. For every man shall bear his own burden. —Gal. 6:4-5

"Mother, will you button my dress?" a child said.

"Do it yourself," said the mother.

"Mother, will you put on my coat?" said the child.

"Do it yourself," said the mother.

"Mother, will you tie my shoes?" said the child.

"Do it yourself," said the mother.

In exasperation the little girl exclaimed, "What would I do without myself?"

Happy is the one who early in life learns to be independent, and holds on to it. We must learn to count upon ourselves in the struggle of life. Friends and loved ones cannot always help us. There comes a time in life when we must make our own decisions and fight our own battles. We must be willing to accept the results of our own choices.

We limit our growth when we cling too close to others. We are unfair to them as well. Trees in a forest which grow too close to one another never develop into strong trees. They grow tall and spindling. A tree which stands alone in an open place produces a sturdy trunk and strong branches.

I pray for strength, dear Lord, to face my own problems today and to conquer them by Thy help.

Read Eph. 3:14-21

He Speaks Again

I can do all things through Christ which strengtheneth me.
—Phil. 4:13

A SOLDIER lost his voice in the war in Korea. He returned to this country for an operation on his throat. Then followed months of endless practice trying to learn to speak again.

As the discouraged veteran walked along the beach by his cottage home one day, he thought of suicide as the quickest way out. A little mongrel pup dropped a piece of driftwood at his feet, begging for a game. The man idly tossed the stick, and the eager dog raced for it. Time and again the pup retrieved it from the beach. Finally the stick landed in the water, and the tide carried it out beyond reach.

Later that evening the man opened his door to find the little pup on his doorstep. It was wet all through, but the piece of wood was in its mouth. The dog had not given up. Neither would the man! Today he speaks again.

Our greatest victories are won little by little, inch by inch. We do not reach the mountaintop in one leap. We climb it step by step. We swim the channel stroke by stroke. It all depends upon our refusal to quit.

Almighty God, give me faith to believe that all things are possible through Thee. May I be numbered among those who cannot be conquered.

Nevertheless

*Nevertheless God, that comforteth those that are cast down,
comforted us by the coming of Titus.   —II Cor. 7:6*

PAUL WAS FORCED back step by step many times in his work of
spreading the gospel. But he always turned back and took a
new grasp on what he had left. He always turned from man
to God, and said, "Nevertheless God."

When Paul went into Macedonia, he said he was weary,
and perplexed on every side by trouble, and fearful of what
might happen. Then he said, "Nevertheless God sent a friend
to me who brought me messages which made my heart rejoice."
Instead of grieving over a bad situation, he still found something to cheer him.

> If there's no Sun, I still can have the Moon;
> If there's no Moon, the Stars my needs suffice;
> And if these fail, I have my Evening Lamp;
> Or, Lampless, there's my trusty Tallow Dip,
> And if the Dip goes out, my Couch remains,
> Where I may sleep and dream there's Light again.
>
> —JOHN KENDRICK BANGS

*My Father, I thank Thee that there is always something for
which I may be thankful. Help me to look for the "nevertheless" blessings of life.*

Burden Bearing

Bear ye one another's burdens, and so fulfill the law of Christ.
—Gal. 6:2

IN CINCINNATI there is a life-size statue of Abraham Lincoln by George Grey Barnard. The sculptor studied Lincoln's death mask ten hours a day for four months. As he told the story to a veteran of World War I, he said, "Burns, do you remember those frightful roads in France, torn by shell, soaked by rain, and then cut deep by wheels of ambulances and guns until all one could find of the road was ruts? That is what I saw in Lincoln's face!"

Soldiers coming home from the battlefields bring in their faces and often in their bodies the marks of the burdens they have borne. Burden bearing is the common lot of all. Jesus' body bore the marks of man's cruelty. Paul said, "I bear in my body the marks of the Lord Jesus." Only the faces of the young or the feeble-minded show no mark of suffering.

Every man must bear his own burden. It fits only his own shoulders because it is made from his own life's experiences. But it may be shared by others. Then the burden becomes light. When we help to bear another's burden, we fulfill the law of Christ.

May I be more willing, O God, to take the burdens of others upon myself. May there be compassion in my heart for all who suffer.

70

Fragments

When they were filled, he said unto his disciples, Gather up the fragments that remain, that nothing be lost. —John 6:12

THE SUPERINTENDENT of the Good Will Industries in a certain city has a beautiful doll in his office. It typifies the work of this institution. This doll was recovered from an ash can in an alley. The rescuer cleaned her up, made her a new wig of yellow yarn, repainted her cheeks, and made her a dress of organdy. She would delight the heart of any little girl.

After feeding five thousand people Jesus said something like this: "Don't throw anything away. Here are baskets. Gather up all the leftovers. We can find some use for them."

The famous mosaics of Europe are made from small pieces of stone or glass fitted together to form a pattern. By themselves they are only fragments. But from the dream of the artist and in his hands they become a glorious work of art.

A catastrophe may shatter our dream of a lifetime. We may see the plans we have cherished through the years melt away and leave only broken bits in our hands.

Let us gather up these fragments and offer them to Jesus. He can show us how to use them. He can help us make something new and beautiful out of them. It may be better than the thing we planned.

Dear Master, use the broken fragments of my life and help me to build anew after Thy pattern.

Songs of Courage

It is a good thing to give thanks unto the Lord, and to sing praises unto thy name, O most High.   —*Ps. 92:1*

A SOLDIER on the battlefield was weary in body and sick at heart from loneliness. In the darkness of night he stole out of camp with his rifle, intending to end his life. Through the darkness he heard the sound of a voice softly singing an old familiar hymn. It was one he remembered from his childhood. Somewhere out there a buddy who was as bad off as he was refused to give in. He still could sing. Courage came back into the soldier's heart as he listened.

God puts songs into our hearts and onto our lips for such purposes as this. When the mind dwells on God, songs break forth in the heart. They lift its burden and renew its courage.

Nothing is too small for which to praise God. Each little joy, each unexpected glimpse of beauty, every thought of Him, should start a song in our hearts. We should fling it out to bless others. Paul tells us to speak to ourselves in psalms and hymns and spiritual songs, and to sing and make melody in our hearts to the Lord.

God of glory, help me to join in the music of Thy creation everywhere. Let the song Thou hast put in my heart overflow and enter into the lives of others.

God Is Always Good

*God is our refuge and strength, a very present help in trouble.
Therefore will not we fear, though the earth be removed, and
though the mountains be carried into the midst of the sea.*
—Ps. 46:1-2

As a young girl living in Kingston, Jamaica, Estelle Carver
saw the city destroyed by a terrible earthquake. She escaped
injury, but her father was buried beneath the ruins of their
home. Rescuers brought out his limp body and laid it on the
lawn. She threw herself upon the still form in an agony of rebellion against God.

"Oh, Daddy," she sobbed, "God isn't good."

Her father stirred slightly. In low words, but with a note of
certainty which banished all doubt and rebellion from her
heart, he expressed his unshaken faith.

"My darling," he said, "God is always good!"

Passing years can bring no greater treasure to the human
heart than the realization that God is always good. Time in-
evitably brings misfortune, loss, and heartache. It is through
the tears of such experiences that the goodness of God shines.
We feel the everlasting arms beneath us. We rest in His love.
"Therefore will not we fear."

*Heavenly Father, I rejoice that I can look into Thy face and
call Thee Father.*

Your Father Knows

Your heavenly Father knoweth that ye have need of all these things.   —Matt. 6:32

DURING A GREAT BATTLE between kings a part of one of the armies was under the command of a young prince. This youth was sorely beset as the battle progressed, and he sent word to his father, asking for help. None came. He sent another messenger. This happened several times. Then the king sent back this message: "Tell my son that I am too good a general not to know when he needs help and too kind a father not to send it when he needs it!"

God's care is always around us. It is over all his creation— the birds of the air, the lilies of the field. It surrounds his children like a mantle. He knows our needs, our wants, our cares. He hears our every cry. Our hearts may rest and our fears may be stilled by this assurance.

> My Father knows, my Father hears,
> My Father sees, my Father cares,
> My Father loves because he knows,
> And knowing all, his love o'erflows;
>   He sees, he hears, he cares, he knows;
>   With love for all his heart o'erflows!
>   —WILBUR FISK TILLETT

My Father, increase my trust in Thy fatherly protection. Today let me rest in Thy care.

Sharing the Load

The eternal God is thy refuge, and underneath are the ever-lasting arms.
　　　　　　　　　　　　　　　　—Deut. 33:27

TWO MEN SAT on the porch one afternoon engaged in conversation. One of them called his little boy to bring him a book from his desk upstairs. When the child did not appear for some time, the father stepped into the house to see what had become of him. He saw the little fellow at the head of the stairs, balancing the heavy book in his arms, afraid to start. With leaping steps, the father reached the top of the stairs. He caught both the child and the book in his arms and brought them safely down.

God's loving arms are always beneath us to support us when we face difficult tasks. If we are called to a strange place, He is our Guide and opens the way for us. If we meet a challenge to our health, He comes as the Great Physician to heal. If we face loneliness from the loss of loved ones, He sustains us with His comfort. If living conditions are difficult, He increases our patience and fortitude.

"Let us therefore come boldly unto the throne of grace, that we may obtain mercy, and find grace to help in time of need."

Everlasting Father, be very near to me now. Let me feel Thy understanding love. I look to Thee for support in every need.

Something Better

Then Peter said, Silver and gold have I none; but such as I have give I thee: In the name of Jesus Christ of Nazareth rise up and walk.   —Acts 3:6

ONE AFTERNOON the two apostles Peter and John went to the temple at the hour of prayer. At the main entrance, "The Beautiful Gate," a lame man sat, begging alms and hoping for small relief from his poverty. Peter, looking upon him, said, "Silver and gold have I none; but such as I have give I thee: In the name of Jesus Christ of Nazareth rise up and walk." In incredible wonder the man stood up! Then walking and leaping and praising God, he went with the apostles into the temple.

We come to our Heavenly Father asking for relief from some temporary want. We do not dare to voice our deeper need. Our faith is so little, our expectations so small. But our Father's storehouse overflows with wealth. He has riches for us we cannot dream of. Instead of giving us a crust of bread, he would give us the power to earn the whole loaf. He wants us to be whole, to run and to leap in newness of life. He can heal our bodies; He can change our hearts; He can make us new creatures.

"According to your faith be it unto you."

O Thou Giver of all good and perfect gifts, supply my unknown needs according to Thy infinite wisdom and love.

Go with God

And Enoch walked with God: and he was not; for God took him.   —Gen. 5:24

"Vaya con Dios"—"Go with God"—the Spanish so beautifully say as they bid good-by to friends.

There is a difference in asking God to be with you as you begin a new day and in asking Him to let you go with Him through the day. Your plans may not be His plans. They may be selfish plans which even you may not realize. And in that sense He cannot bless them. When you say, "Father, today I will walk with Thee into whatever paths Thou wilt lead me. I will follow Thee in word and deed. Show me Thy way," then you make His guidance possible.

To go with God means to trust Him. You may not see why He leads you where He does. The way may not be easy or attractive. You may shrink from the strangeness of it. You may long for another and more pleasant way.

In *Pilgrim's Progress* as Christian approached the beautiful palace he met Timorous and Mistrust, who had turned back because they said that two lions blocked the road ahead. Christian continued on his way in spite of fear. When he came to the lions, he found that they were chained. And he entered the palace unhurt.

My Father, today I put my hand in Thine. I shall walk safely with Thee.

77

God's World

The Lord is my rock, and my fortress, and my deliverer; the God of my rock; in him will I trust: he is my shield, and the horn of my salvation, my high tower, and my refuge, my saviour; thou savest me from violence.   —II Sam. 22:2-3

DURING WORLD WAR II an air raid siren sounded a practice signal. All lights were extinguished, and a family gathered on the lawn to watch the lights go out in the neighborhood.

Suddenly the little daughter exclaimed, "Daddy, what shall we do about the fireflies? How can we put them out?"

"They belong to God," he said; "we can never put them out."

We should stop occasionally to remind ourselves that we live in God's world. Man has brought destruction and grief into it, but it still belongs to God. He gives us power to overcome the evil when we are willing to co-operate with Him.

> The moon rose up the wintry sky,
>   The great full moon unearthly bright.
> "The bomber's moon," said one who watched.
>   "There'll be dark wings abroad tonight."
>
> .   .   .   .
>
> In the unplumbed, uncharted blue
>   Where all time waits nor life has trod,
> A still wind stirred to touch the earth.
>   "Whose moon?" said God.
>
> —FANNY HEASLIP LEA

My refuge is in Thee, O Lord. Of whom shall I be afraid?

Hidden Power

He shall cover thee with his feathers, and under his wings shalt thou trust: his truth shall be thy shield and buckler.—Ps. 91:4

IN THE HIMALAYA MOUNTAINS the natives work in deep snows at high altitudes. One wonders how they are able to endure the cold. It is said that each man wears suspended around his neck a small vase in which is placed a piece of glowing charcoal. This is hidden by his clothes, but it acts as a little heater to warm him.

Often we see men and women battled by the great storms of life. They go calmly on, upheld and fortified by some invisible power. They carry close to their hearts something that enables them to rise above the hardest blows. They have found the secret of strength. They know through experience that they do not walk alone. There is an unseen Companion who goes with them.

John the Baptist preached, saying, "There cometh one mightier than I after me, the latchet of whose shoes I am not worthy to stoop down and unloose." To know that mightier One is to know the secret of power. His strength will supplement your strength. What you cannot do, He will do for you. When your wisdom ends, His will take over. You will be sufficient for whatever comes.

Almighty God, I look to Thee for strength to meet my every need.

Give Up Worry

Cast thy burden upon the Lord, and he shall sustain thee: he shall never suffer righteousness to be moved.—Ps.55:22

BISHOP QUAYLE tells of a night in his life when he had worried far into the early hours over a perplexing problem. He said finally he heard God's voice speaking to him, saying, "Quayle, you go to bed. I'll sit up the rest of the night." He released his worry and went to sleep. In the morning the solution to his problem was clear to him.

Almost everyone who has reached middle life has some burden too great to bear alone. It may be a secret worry which others do not know. But God never meant us to carry our burden alone. He says, "Come unto me, all ye that labour and are heavy laden, and I will give you rest." He offers to share the load with us.

In despair sometimes we turn to Him and ask for help. Then we pick up our load and place it upon our shoulders again and stumble on.

When we have done all we are capable of doing for ourselves, we may cast our care upon Him. We may leave it with Him. We may trust Him to take care of it for us in His own good time.

O Thou Great Burden-bearer of the race, I bring my care to Thee. I thank Thee that Thou wilt share it with me.

Unused Resources

My God shall supply all your need according to his riches in glory by Christ Jesus.   —Phil. 4:19

JOHN R. MOTT has said, "With a deepening sense of humiliation let us dwell on our unused resources. How comparatively unused are the capacities of heart-power, of statesmanship, of unselfishness, of saintliness, of adventure, of heroism, of sacrifice, of fellowship and unity."

No person lives up to his highest capacities. Only a small part of the brain has been developed even in persons whom we call geniuses. In the spiritual realm this is true to a much greater degree. We have yet to see what we may become when we tap the limitless power of God. There are riches of power in Christ Jesus. He is longing to give them to us if our faith and dedication are only big enough. They are superhuman resources.

In whatever place or condition we find ourselves these resources are available. They can meet any need. Do we need patience to meet the daily annoyances which plague our steps? Do we need courage to bear our suffering and pain? Do we need new hope to start again in the face of our losses? We need never walk alone. We may draw upon the mighty resources of God. Through the Holy Spirit these spiritual energies may be ours.

My Father, I will draw upon Thy mighty power for all my need.

Great Gladness

Then were the disciples glad, when they saw the Lord.
                                        —John 20:20

ON THE OLD BATTLEFIELD of Waterloo stands a circular building. A painting covers the entire inside circumference of the building. It shows in detail the various stages of the battle. The central figure in the painting is Napoleon, mounted on his white charger. The men who fought under him came to believe him to be resistless. When he appeared on his white charger before his troops, confidence flashed down the line of his men. They became mighty as soldiers had seldom been mighty before.

The appearance of Jesus after the resurrection inspired his disciples with a mighty confidence. It made them invincible. It filled them with a great gladness.

Jesus saith unto them, "Peace be unto you." This was something more than the familiar greeting of friend to friend. It was not merely a kind word to pacify their fears. It had larger meaning. These disciples needed confidence for the days ahead. Jesus would not leave them until he was sure they had it.

Jesus wanted His disciples to know that the same power which had raised Him from the dead was behind them. They could use it in the days of kingdom building. They could move forward with a sense of victory in their hearts.

I thank Thee, O Christ, that Thy presence means gladness and victory in my life.

Reshaping the Pattern

And the vessel that he made of clay was marred in the hand of the potter: so he made it again another vessel, as seemed good to the potter to make it.   —Jer. 18:4

THE ARTIST SIR HUBERT VON HERKOMER was the son of a wood-carver in the Black Forest of Germany. When he rose to fame, he established his studio in London and brought his father to live with him. The old man spent his time modeling clay. Finally his hands lost their cunning. He often went to bed sad at heart, thinking his best days were gone. The son detected this. When his father was asleep, he would rework the clay with his own wonderful skill. In the morning when the old man took up his work again he was overjoyed, and exclaimed, "I can do it as well as ever I did."

This is what God is continually doing for His children. He takes the imperfect work of our hands and remakes it into something beautiful and useful.

Our lives are in God's hands. He has an ideal for each life. When we resist His will and spoil the pattern, He does not give us up. He helps us begin over again and reshape the pattern. He is continually at work making new men out of broken and marred ones. He is never satisfied until He has produced the best possible out of the material in His hands. "He made it again another vessel."

My Father, wilt Thou remake me after Thy perfect pattern. "Thou art the potter, I am the clay."

83

Stand Fast

Watch ye, stand fast in the faith, quit ye like men, be strong.
—I Cor. 16:13

MR. STAND-FAST was one of Bunyan's famous pilgrims. He was the last one to cross the river of Death. The messenger who came to summon him spoke in tender words, saying, "The Master is not willing that you should be so far from him any longer." While this pilgrim was crossing the river, there was a great calm. He stood for a time in midstream talking with friends who were watching from the shore. He assured them that the river had no terrors at all. He found the journey peaceful and pleasant.

A man must have some settled convictions in life. This is especially true in regard to his religious faith. Otherwise he wastes too much time re-examining his beliefs. Life is not long enough for that. If a man would do his lifework well and help others, he must fix himself upon certain great beliefs, and then stand fast.

We must hold to our faith in Jesus Christ with all our heart and mind. We must be rooted and grounded in it. Deep roots produce growth and fruit.

Our steadfast faith helps to build faith in weaker hearts. It is worth while to do that for someone else. "Be thou faithful unto death, and I will give thee a crown of life."

O God, enable me to hold fast to my faith that I may win the crown of life from Thy hand.

Hold on to Faith

Be merciful unto me, O God, be merciful unto me: for my
soul trusteth in thee: yea, in the shadow of thy wings will I make
my refuge, until these calamities be overpast.   —Ps. 57:1

DURING THE WAR two storekeepers in England had their store
fronts bombed away. Next morning one repaired his entrance
as best he could by bits of broken tin, lumber, and glass that he
found near by. He put up a sign, "Open as usual." The other
man's store front was in much worse condition. It was beyond
repair for the time. But the man just smiled and put up a sign,
"More open than usual."

Nothing is hopeless if we hold on to faith. Doubt and despair
have no place in a Christian's heart. They defeat us before we
start. Life will not be easy all the way. We must expect
trouble. It is sure to come. The road twists and turns; there are
always the hilltop and the bogland. But as long as we hold on
to faith and hope, nothing can defeat us.

> Behold, we know not anything;
>   I can but trust that good shall fall
>   At last—far off—at last, to all,
> And every winter change to spring.
>   —ALFRED TENNYSON

Light within me, Lord, a faith that cannot be destroyed. Give
me courage to believe when I cannot see.

The Morning Has Come!

Whereby are given unto us exceeding great and precious promises: that by these ye might be partakers of the divine nature.   —II Pet. 1:4

IN ONE of Will Rogers' moving pictures he plays the part of a country doctor. He goes to the bedside of a dying child, the only son of a poor widow. Before he leaves, he tells her that if the child lives until morning he will get well. The following morning he returns to find her sitting in the darkened room, the lamp still burning.

"How is he?" she asks.

The doctor throws open the blinds and says, "The morning has come!"

Our Father has given us many wonderful promises. We know these promises, but we act as if we had never heard them. He says He will never leave us, yet we are lonely. He says He will provide for us even down to old age, yet we fear that poverty may overtake us. He says He will forgive our sins and remember them no more, yet we torment ourselves over failures of the past. Jesus tells us if we believe in Him we shall never die, yet we fear death and mourn for those who are gone.

Let us believe His word. Let us throw open our hearts and let the sunshine of our Father's love come flooding in.

My Father, Thy promises are a rock upon which I may plant my feet. Help me to claim these promises for my own.

Beauty for Ashes

To give unto them beauty for ashes, the oil of joy for mourn-
ing, the garment of praise for the spirit of heaviness; that they
might be called trees of righteousness, the planting of the Lord,
that he might be glorified.   —*Isa. 61:3*

"GARLAND" IS USED for the word "beauty" in the revised ver-
sions. Thus the figure is of a person bowed in grief and crouch-
ing beside the road pouring ashes over his head. Then there
comes by someone who lifts the mourner from the dust, wipes
away his ashes, and places instead a wreath of flowers upon
his head.

Many men, often Christians, travel through life beset with
fears, burdened with care, and faced with defeat. They do not
know, or they forget, that One walks besides them who is
able to transform life into a shining path, and able to satisfy the
deepest longings of the heart.

We come to Him in our blindness, and He gives us sight.
We bring Him our sorrow, and He gives us joy. We come in
trouble, and we find peace. We come in our poverty, and we
take from Him wealth. We bring Him our lives which are faced
with death and defeat, and we receive from Him life and victory.

Gracious Lord, grant that I may realize today that in Thee
is all the fullness of life, and that Thou art ready to fill me with
Thy power.

Still Learning

Surely goodness and mercy shall follow me all the days of my life: and I will dwell in the house of the Lord for ever.

—Ps. 23:6

"STILL I AM LEARNING," said Michelangelo at the age of eighty.

Passing years may rob a man of physical strength, but they have little power to diminish his spiritual capacities. Many of the great accomplishments of the world have been performed by men in later life. Tennyson wrote "Crossing the Bar" at eighty. Goethe wrote "Faust" at eighty. Gladstone was prime minister of England at eighty-five.

If our lives become dull and routine, it is because we have ceased to make an effort to grow. Each one of us is capable of engaging in some form of creative activity. We may fashion some bit of lovely handwork; we may learn the art of flower arrangement, or discover the charm of ceramics.

> For age is opportunity no less
> Than youth itself, though in another dress,
> And as the evening twilight fades away
> The sky is filled with stars, invisible by day.
>
> *—HENRY W. LONGFELLOW*

O Thou great Teacher, fill my mind with new truth today. Give me a desire to keep on learning.

Always Young

*But whosoever drinketh of the water that I shall give him
shall never thirst; but the water that I shall give him shall be in
him a well of water springing up into everlasting life.*
                                                        —John 4:14

DR. LILLIEN MARTIN, head of the Old Age Counselling Center
in San Francisco when she was over ninety years old, led hundreds of older men and women to happiness by showing them
how to return to active life. She was an example of what she
taught. At sixty-five she retired from teaching and established
one of the first child guidance clinics in America. She learned
to drive a car at the age of seventy-six, and drove across the
continent six times. She circled the world twice. At eighty-seven
she traveled twenty thousand miles through cities and jungles
in South America.

"Be interested and alive to the world," she said, "for in
boredom and ennui lies true old age."

Age is a matter of feeling and not of the calendar or of appearance. A real interest in other people and a habit of doing
little acts of kindness keep one youthful and happy.

Two women were discussing a third who had just left them.
One said, "How old do you think she is?"

"Why, I don't know," replied the other. "I was so interested
in what she was doing and saying, I never thought of that."

*Father of all, may I never lose my zest for living or my in-
terest in my fellow men.*

89

Life as a Whole

Lord, make me to know mine end, and the measure of my days.   —*Ps.* 39:4

AN AUTOMOBILE must have both a windshield and a rear-view mirror. The large windshield gives a view of the road ahead. The small mirror shows the road just traveled. The careful driver uses both to view the whole road. Thus he arrives safely at his destination.

As we journey along life's road, we need to use both windshield and rear-view mirror. We should think of life as a whole, with problems much the same as we go along. We face responsibilities, sorrows, losses at all ages. We must meet them upon the level of our understanding and development.

It is a mistake to pigeonhole life and label it in separate parts. Formerly when a lady reached fifty years she changed her mode of dress as well as her activities. She put on a cap and shawl, and retired to the rocking chair. Today it is not always easy to tell mother from daughter. Grandmothers may be as active in life's affairs as their children.

> . . . A whole I planned,
> Youth shows but half; trust God:
> see all, nor be afraid!
>
> —ROBERT BROWNING

God of all life, guard me from the temptation to withdraw from life. Help me to take my part in its work and play.

Longevity

And all the days of Methuselah were nine hundred sixty and nine years: and he died.
—Gen. 5:27

A BRITISH SERGEANT in World War I shouted to his cowering men, "Come on! Do you want to live forever?"

A long life is not primarily of great importance. It may or may not be a blessing to a person. It depends upon what is done with that life. It is a question of not how long you live but how you live.

The Bible records only one fact about Methuselah's life as being worthy of mention. It was the number of his days on earth. There is no mention of any other achievement. Did he have any breadth of interest, any depth of conviction, any height of aspiration? Nobody knows. He just lived nine hundred and sixty-nine years and died.

Jesus Christ lived only a few years, but he changed the whole course of human history. Life to him meant an opportunity to love and serve. Methuselah lived long; Jesus lived well.

> We live in deeds, not years; in thoughts, not breaths;
> In feelings, not in figures on a dial.
> We should count time by heart-throbs. He most lives
> Who thinks most, feels noblest, acts the best.
>
> —PHILIP JAMES BAILEY

Help me, O God, to live richly and creatively, and to give myself completely to the cause of Christ.

Vistas

*Thou wilt shew me the path of life: in thy presence is fulness
of joy; at thy right hand there are pleasures for evermore.*
—Ps. 16:11

"HALF THE BEAUTY of a garden lies in its vistas," says Dwight
Farnham, an authority on gardens. "Foreign gardens are always
filled with vistas. There are vistas down marble stairways,
through age-old trees. Always at the end there is something
beautiful to see, such as a view, a fountain, a pool, a statue, or
a rose-covered ruin, something which makes you want to trav-
erse that tunnel to the end."

The path of our life is something like a vista or a tunnel. It
stretches through a bordered way but opens out in the end
into something beautiful. Why not take this long view of life?
When we are beset with duties and burdens, let us lift our eyes
to see the beauty at the end of the road. It sheds a light over the
way. Bitter experiences of the present do not seem so hard
when we keep our eyes on the goal.

God seemingly withholds the answer to many prayers. Let
us not give up hope. We will find the answer some day. The
soldier receives his medal only when the battle is over. The
laborer must come home for his hire.

*Help me, my Father, to keep my eyes upon Thee as I journey
toward the heavenly city.*

Enthusiasm for Life

Whatsoever thy hand findeth to do, do it with thy might.
—*Eccl. 9:10*

"FOLKS WONDER how I've kept so young," said Luther Burbank, the great horticulturist. "I'm almost seventy-seven, and I can still go over a gate or run a foot-race or kick the chandelier. That's because my body is no older than my mind—my mind is adolescent. It has never grown up. . . . I'm as inquisitive as I was at eight."

For five years we lived as neighbors to Luther Burbank, who at that time was in the last years of life. We watched him at his work among his plants and flowers in his experimental grounds. His keen eye noticed each tiny plant development. He waited with infinite patience for each repeated graft to change the nature of a flower or tree. He worked all day long.

He was interested in his friends and neighbors, in the civic life of his town, and in the development of children. He made a notable contribution to each of these. Everything challenged his interest and compassion. He never grew old.

Enthusiasm is an earnestness joined with faith and courage and hope. It overcomes hindrances of the world. It brings to pass wondrous things. It puts a thrill into the heart.

God of infinite wisdom, help me to hold on to the wonder of life. Never let me lose a zest for discovery.

Holy Ground

The place whereon thou standest is holy ground.—Exod. 3:5

DURING THE LAST WORLD WAR a young musician from England was interned in a prison camp. During that time he composed an eight-part choral and won his Doctorate of Music at Oxford University.

All of us are prone to think at times that we could be happier if we lived in another place and under other conditions. We blame our discontent upon our surroundings. We excuse our ill temper by condemning those about us.

Happiness never comes from without. It always comes from within. If we cannot be happy in the place we are, we will never be happy any other place. Happiness comes from the love of God in our hearts and the security it brings.

The place where we live is holy ground when we realize that God is with us there. If the surroundings are not what we want them to be, we can make of them an opportunity for growth. When we have mastered the present lesson, God will open a new door for us, perhaps in other places and conditions. Our journey with Him moves ever onward with new opportunities and joys when we are ready for them. Our task for today is to live on holy ground where we are.

My Father, let me remember that Thou art with me and that I live on holy ground. May I know that every experience is an opportunity for growth.

The Disciplined Heart

But I say unto you, That ye resist not evil: but whosoever shall smite thee on thy right cheek, turn to him the other also.
—Matt. 5:39

WHILE ROBERT E. LEE was a cadet at West Point, a classmate took a violent dislike to him. This feeling persisted through the years. The fellow officer made many attacks upon Lee.

One day an acquaintance asked Lee what he thought of the man. Lee spoke of him in highest terms.

"You must not know what he has been saying about you for years," the man said.

"You did not ask me what this man thought of me," Lee replied, "but what was my opinion of him."

Great souls live above the attacks of little men. They refuse to descend to the level of ungenerous thinking. They ignore unkindness and refuse to answer back.

The miracle and contagion of Christlike lives lies in this fact. They see the good in others because of the good in their own lives. They are everyone's friend because of their friendship with the Master. They are winsome because they have been won by Him.

So few of us live up to this ideal. Our hearts need a new discipline of love. All of us may have it.

Heavenly Father, if I have failed to live above the petty annoyances of life, I ask Thee to forgive me. Teach me self-mastery.

The Forgiving Heart

And be ye kind one to another, tenderhearted, forgiving one another, even as God for Christ's sake hath forgiven you.
—Eph. 4:32

A WOMAN became offended at the pastor and members of a little church where she had been a member all her life. She never again entered the church. As age came on, she gradually lost her eyesight and finally became bedfast. In her physical darkness God's love shone into her heart. She called the members of the church to come to her and asked forgiveness of them. The radiance of God lighted up her face, for her heart was at peace once more.

Jesus was so sure that a forgiving attitude is necessary that He included it in the basic petitions He taught his disciples to pray: "Forgive us . . . as we forgive." One of His great parables deals with the man who would not forgive his fellow servant after his own debts had been forgiven by his master. God could not forgive this man because his own unforgiving heart had shut God out.

Peter asked Jesus how many times he should forgive his brother who had sinned against him. Jesus replied, "Until seventy times seven." In other words, there can be no limit for the forgiving heart.

Give me a forgiving heart, gracious Lord, that I may have the right to ask forgiveness of Thee.

Little Resentments

Let all bitterness, and wrath, and anger, and clamour, and evil speaking, be put away from you, with all malice.

—*Eph. 4:31*

ONE EVENING the gears in my car jammed, and I could not shift it out of low gear. I could not back it up or make it pick up any speed. The grinding of the motor wore on my nerves and patience. My little car, which usually bounded over the road, was lame. The joy of the road was gone.

Little resentments carried in the heart against another jam the gears of life and destroy the joy of living. If we allow them to grow, they destroy not only joy but ourselves as well. Resentments are little hates which fester in the heart and break out in irritability, ill temper, and self-pity. They make it impossible for one to love or be loved. Even if some resentments may seem to be justified, we must rid ourselves of them and forgive and forget as soon as possible.

"Anger," someone has said, "is the punishment we inflict upon ourselves because of the wrongdoing of another." If we do not do away with it, we shut ourselves off even from the love of God. Jesus said, "If ye forgive not men their trespasses, neither will your Father forgive your trespasses." It is impossible to love God and hate our fellow man.

Cleanse me, O Father, from all resentment, hate, ill temper, and self-pity. Help me to be tenderhearted and forgiving.

Let God Judge

Judge not according to the appearance, but judge righteous judgment.   *—John 7:24*

"STEPPING HEAVENWARD" was a popular religious book a generation ago. It is the life story, told in diary form, of a girl's struggle in the Christian life. She resented particularly a habit of her aged father-in-law. Periodically he locked himself in his room and refused to come out for his meals. After his death she found out by reading his diary that he had spent those days alone in fasting and prayer for her and her family. She had thought him to be selfish and obstinate. Instead he had tried in his own way to bless her and her household.

When we do not understand the reason behind what other people do, it is better to reserve judgment. It is better still to place upon their acts a kind motive. Only God completely understands each one of us. He "looketh on the heart" and understands why we do as we do. We may judge others only by the outward appearance. That is not enough. So leave it with God.

Tolerance of those about us is a beautiful sign of maturity in Christian character. It does not condemn another unheard. It refuses to blame even when it cannot agree with what another does.

Dear Lord, I would be free from judging others. I would leave that to Thy unerring wisdom.

Judging to Help

Why dost thou judge thy brother? or why dost thou set at nought thy brother?   *—Rom. 14:10*

WHEN WOODROW WILSON was in Versailles after World War I, fighting for the principles of the League of Nations, it is reported that the French statesman Clemenceau said, "He talks like Jesus Christ."

The world is in trouble today because men and women do not talk like Jesus Christ. There is a casual and superficial interest in another's affairs which leads to gossip and criticism. There are many things in other people's lives which are wholly no concern of ours. We have no right to know about them, or to discuss them with our neighbors.

It is quite another thing to listen willingly and sympathetically to others who come to us for help. We may help another greatly by being an understanding listener and by keeping confidences imposed in us.

"A man shall be as an hiding place from the wind, and a covert from the tempest; as rivers of water in a dry place, as the shadow of a great rock in a weary land."

Do you mean that to other people?

Do they turn to you for help and understanding in time of need?

Help me, O God, to judge another only so that I may help him. Help me to talk like Jesus Christ.

Appreciate the Good

They say unto him, Master, this woman was taken in adultery, in the very act. . . . What sayest thou? But Jesus stooped down, and with his finger wrote on the ground, as though he heard them not. —John 8:4-6

HENRY WARD BEECHER, the great preacher, once said, "Have a good word for everyone, or else keep silent."

The Pharisees brought a woman taken in adultery to Jesus and asked Him if she should not be stoned. Jesus did not seem to hear their accusations. He stooped down and "with his finger wrote on the ground, as though he heard them not."

Jesus had no use for gossip or talebearing. When his enemies accused Him falsely, He remained silent. The surest way to silence gossip is to refuse to listen to it or to repeat it.

The psalmist prayed, "Set a watch, O Lord, before my mouth; keep the door of my lips." He knew perhaps the temptation to build himself up by running someone else down. He may have known how easy it is to talk about one's neighbors.

Nearly everyone seeks to do the best he can. It is better to see in others their potential power for good than to criticize them for their shortcomings. If we do not understand, let us pray for insight. When we understand, we do not blame.

My Father, help me to be charitable and to praise people for what they do, and not criticize them for what they cannot do. Help me to forgive and to forget the faults of others.

"Is Your Grain Good?"

Behold, how good and how pleasant it is for brethren to dwell together in unity!
                                                                —Ps. 133:1

TWO MEN were discussing the merits of the various branches of the Christian Church. One man was certain that there was but one acceptable road to God. His friend said to him, "For twenty years my son and I have been hauling our grain to the mill over yonder hill. Never once in these years has the miller inquired by which road we came. But he has always asked, 'Is your grain good?' "

The things in life which divide men are usually not the essential things. They are like the fences which divide the newly seeded farm lands. In the spring they stand out in bold square pattern. In the autumn of the year one no longer sees the fences but the spreading harvest which covers all dividing lines. It is the harvest which counts. Is it a good harvest?

> Yes, we do differ when we most agree,
> For words are not the same to you and me,
> And it may be our several spiritual needs
> Are best supplied by seeming different creeds.
>   *—HARTLEY COLERIDGE*

Father of all, help me to consider the heart and not the label a man wears. Teach me to grow in tolerance for all people.

101

Read I Cor. 13

Growing in Love

And this I pray, that your love may abound yet more and more in knowledge and in all judgment. —Phil. 1:9

E. STANLEY JONES writes, "But in all our growth we must grow in love. Unless we are growing in love, we are not growing at all." Love is the answer to the world's need. Jesus loved men when He walked among them. He loved them most when He died for them on the cross. Real love is sacrificial. Its highest expression is in giving. God so loved that He gave His Son. Jesus so loved that He gave His life.

It is natural for us to love our families and our friends. It is not always easy to love all people. Christ's love in our hearts makes it possible.

I ask Thee for a thoughtful love,
Through constant watching wise,
To meet the glad with joyful smiles,
And wipe the weeping eyes,
And a heart, at leisure from itself,
To soothe and sympathize.
—ANNA LAETITIA WARING

I would grow day by day in love, my Father. Give me a love more like Thine.

A Bridge of Love

A new commandment I give unto you, That ye love one another; as I have loved you, that ye also love one another. By this shall all men know that ye are my disciples, if ye have love one to another.   *—John 13:34-35*

BEAUTIFUL GOLDEN GATE BRIDGE spans the entrance to San Francisco Bay. It is anchored in mighty towers on either side of the gateway. The foundations of these towers go deep into the rock ribs of the earth; their tops are often shrouded in the clouds. The bridge may sway from the ocean gales, but it stands secure. It forms a safe passageway for the traffic which flows in endless stream across its surface.

A young Chinese bride in San Francisco said of one of the deaconesses of her church, "She built a bridge of love from her heart to mine, and Jesus walked across."

Christian love is translated by the Greek word *agape*. It means a love so great and constant that it redeems the one who is loved. Jesus showed us the limits to which that kind of love will go when He died on the cross. He built a safe bridge between men and their Heavenly Father.

When love controls our lives, we open a passageway over which other men may find God.

Use my life today, Father, as a safe bridge over which someone may find Thee.

Read Mark 12:28-34

Outgoing Love

Thou shalt love the Lord thy God with all thy heart, and with all thy soul, and with all thy mind, and with all thy strength. This is the first commandment. And the second is like, namely this, Thou shalt love thy neighbour as thyself.   —Mark 12:30-31

THÉOBALD CHARTRAN painted a picture entitled "St. Francis Singing." Francis is plowing with a team of immense oxen. The hillside is bare and stony. The oxen strain at their task. Francis' back is bent as he leans heavily on the plow handle. Crows fly over the field, ready to pounce upon the seed as soon as it is scattered. But Francis' face is turned toward the sun, and he is singing.

Francis gave up a home of wealth and influence to live in poverty, tending the poor and sick, and preaching simply to all who would hear him. Legends adorn his life with charming incidents of his love for all living creatures. Birds rested in his arms; little wild rabbits ran to him for protection.

This kind of love comes from one who walks close to God. God's own love flows through such a life and blesses all His creation. It encircles men of all nations and stations. It includes all living things—the birds of the air and the beasts of the field. Is this your kind of love?

Teach me, my Father, that love is the greatest thing in the world. Increase my love for all Thy creation.

Love in Deeds and Seeds

Whoso hath this world's good, and seeth his brother have need, and shutteth up his bowels of compassion from him, how dwelleth the love of God in him? My little children, let us not love in word, neither in tongue; but in deed and in truth.

—I John 3:17-18

SEEDS MAY BECOME DEEDS. A certain man in the United States collects vegetable seeds from all over the country. He solicits them from service clubs, schools, and charitable organizations. When he has gathered thousands of pounds of them, he boards a ship for the various war-ravaged countries of the earth— Korea, China, Japan, Germany. He distributes them to the needy people of these lands. He helps them to help themselves. On later trips the grateful people show him their growing crops and harvest stored for future use.

It is easy to feel compassion for people of other countries who suffer from the ravages of war. It is not so easy to do something about it. It takes trouble to collect warm clothing and pack a box. It takes time to carry it to the post office and send it on its way. But it proves our love.

Jesus had this in mind when He told His disciples to visit the sick, feed the hungry, clothe the naked, welcome the stranger, and minister to those in prison. He said that this is the standard by which each man's life will be tested. Real love expresses itself in deeds.

Enable me, O Lord, to translate my love into action.

Read Luke 10:30-37

Your Brother

*The Lord said unto Cain, Where is Abel thy brother? And he
said, I know not: Am I my brother's keeper?   —Gen. 4:9*

AT THE ENTRANCE of the famous Boys' Town in Nebraska there
is a simple plaque showing the picture of a sturdy young boy
carrying a crippled little boy in his arms. Beneath this is written, "He ain't heavy, Father. He's my brother."

Two men stood looking at the picture. One of them said, "If
only everyone would stand before his God, helping another,
and say, 'He ain't heavy, Father. He's my brother.' "

One of the most beautiful words in our language is brother.
It means strength, protection, loyalty, comradeship. A brother
is one who means more than an acquaintance. He feels an
obligation for your welfare. He puts your good above his own.
You feel free to turn to him in time of need. When we think of
our Lord as our Elder Brother, we are able to understand the
true meaning of the word.

> O brother man! fold to thy heart thy brother;
>   Where pity dwells, the peace of God is there;
> To worship rightly is to love each other,
>   Each smile a hymn, each kindly deed a prayer.
> —JOHN GREENLEAF WHITTIER

*Dear Lord, may I have a greater feeling of brotherhood for
all the lives which touch mine today.*

My Opportunity

Jesus called them unto him, and said, Suffer little children to come unto me, and forbid them not: for of such is the kingdom of God.   *—Luke 18:16*

HEAVEN OFFERS no greater joy than to acquaint a little child with his Heavenly Father.

> My opportunity! Dear Lord, I do not ask
>   That thou shouldst give me some high work of thine
> Some noble calling, or some wondrous task—
>   Give me a little hand to hold in mine.
>
> I do not ask that I should ever stand
>   Among the wise, the worthy, or the great;
> I only ask that softly, hand in hand,
>   A child and I may enter at thy gate.
>
> Give me a little child to point the way
>   Over the strange sweet path that leads to thee;
> Give me a little voice to teach to pray;
>   Give me two shining eyes thy face to see.
>
> I do not need to ask for more than this.
>   My opportunity! 'Tis standing at my door.
> What sorrow if this blessing I should miss!
>   A little child! Why should I ask for more?

—MARION B. CRAIG

Lord, help me to use this opportunity.

The Story Hour

Whoso shall receive one such little child in my name receiveth me.   —Matt. 18:5

THERE IS a painting which shows Jesus seated in a garden with a group of little children gathered around Him. One child is standing at His knee, looking at Jesus' hand. Beneath the picture are the words, "How did you get that scar in your hand?"

If the radio and television of the present day rob little children of the twilight story hour, it will be a great loss. The bedtime story is one of the treasured memories of childhood. Its glow never fades from the heart. We should make a definite effort to preserve this tradition for little children.

That is the hour of questions, of confidences, of lasting influences. The wax is soft and the impressions go deep in their hearts. That is the hour of leading little children into the friendship of the One altogether lovely.

There is a woman who welcomes little children of her neighborhood to her porch on summer evenings for a story hour. She reads them Bible stories and nature stories and fairy tales. They reward her with shining eyes and the words, "Read it again."

Dear Father, when I receive a little child into my heart, I receive Thee. I open my heart to them and Thee.

Giving a Child a Home

Are they not all ministering spirits?—Heb. 1:14

A YOUNG MINISTER and his wife found that they could not have children. They then decided to adopt a family. As it was difficult to get an American child, they chose a child of another nationality. They followed this plan until now they have eight adopted children of various nationalities.

Little children need love more than anything else the world can give. When they are denied the comfort of a mother's arms, their spirits are chilled and their hearts are hardened. Most of the pain and evil in the world is caused by men and women who were denied love and protection in childhood. They live to express their resentment on others.

If we open our hearts and homes to little children, whether for a day or a lifetime, we are doing what Jesus would do. He opened His arms to them in the long ago. Today He would take each homeless little one and place it in some childless home.

> And he who gives a child a treat
> Makes joy-bells ring in Heaven's street,
> And he who gives a child a home
> Builds palaces in Kingdom come.
>
> —JOHN MASEFIELD

Dear Father, fill me with love and hope and patience that I may be a blessing to some little child.

A New Hobby

Remember ye not the former things, neither consider the things of old. Behold, I will do a new thing.—Isa. 43:18-19

A SEVEN-YEAR-OLD BOY and his grandmother appeared together one night on television in a xylophone duet. The grandmother had given the xylophone to the boy and provided lessons for him. While trying to help him in his practice, she decided to learn to play also. She bought an instrument and took lessons. Now the two of them appear together on programs and share the fun of a new accomplishment.

A new hobby creates a new interest in life. It can fill vacancies left by the passing of other joys. It can open up a new world of wonder and excitement. It may reveal a talent you never dreamed you had.

There is double pleasure in a hobby that may be shared with another, especially with a child. A grandparent has much to give in wisdom and patience to children. They will return it in trust and love. Anyone may become a grandparent, not always by nature, but always by adoption. For the world is full of children who need the fairy touch of a godmother. When you find a new hobby, look for a child to share it with you.

Create in me, O God, a desire for new experiences. May I find joy each day in attempting some work for Thee.

Co-operation

So we, being many, are one body in Christ, and every one members one of another.   —Rom. 12:5

IN BENTON, ILLINOIS, there are many old oil wells which until recently were almost dry. A new system was developed which raised the output of oil from a few hundred to thousands of barrels a day. Water is pumped into the well under pressure. It mixes with the remaining oil and sends it to the surface. But one cannot tell where in the field the oil will be forced up. It is necessary for the owners of all the wells to work together and to share alike in the profits.

By co-operation with others each one of us can strengthen his own output of good in the world. The cure for cancer will probably never be found by one man working alone in his own laboratory. When enough people unite their small contributions of money and enough scientists pool their discoveries, the secret will be found. Perhaps neither you nor I will discover the formula for peace this world needs so desperately. But all of us may unite our prayers, our gifts, and our influence to create an attitude which will bring it about.

"We are labourers together with God"—together with one another and then together with Him.

Give me, O Father, a willingness to co-operate with others in daily living.

Humility

For I say, through the grace given unto me, to every man that is among you, not to think of himself more highly than he ought to think. —Rom. 12:3

OVER THE GRAVE of the poet Christina Rossetti in Highgate, England, are inscribed the words from one of her poems:

> Give me the lowest place; or if for me
>   That lowest place too high, make one more low
> Where I may sit and see
>   My God and love Thee so.

When we measure ourselves by Jesus, we become humble. His life is the mirror in which we see ourselves as we really are. Jesus was humble because he was great. Little men are afraid to be humble. They are afraid they will be overlooked or unappreciated. They feel the need to build up their self-importance.

Jesus' humility was rooted in confidence in God. The record says that Jesus, "knowing that the Father had given all things into his hands, and that he was come from God, and went to God, . . . began to wash the disciples' feet.

He gave us a new set of values. He said, "Whosoever will be chief among you, let him be your servant."

My Father, teach me the true humility that was found in Jesus, that I may serve in His spirit.

112

The Smallest Service

*They had a few small fishes: and he blessed, and commanded
to set them also before them. So they did eat, and were filled.*
—Mark 8:7-8

IN THE COLOSSEUM in Los Angeles, California, there are 104,-
000 seats. People filled the seats in this great stadium one night
to hear a noted speaker. He spoke of the importance of each
person's life. Then he asked that all lights in the stadium be
turned off. In the darkness he took a box of matches from his
pocket and lighted a single match. Everyone in the vast crowd
could see the tiny light. Then he asked that everyone light a
match and hold it up. Thousands of little flames lighted up the
arena.

No service is too small to offer God. Each beautiful thing in
the world is made up of tiny parts. All parts blend to make a
perfect whole. Life is composed of small units of time, of individual acts. We live one day at a time, one moment at a
time. The loving thought, the helping hand, the friendly word
of praise, are the things that all can give. Taken all together,
these small gifts become great. They lift the spirit and put new
hope in the heart.

God does not ask some great service from you. He asks only
that it be loving and that it be your best. The very poor may
be lavish with these gifts.

*My Father, to give abundantly of every gift I possess is my
prayer.*

113

Something to Share

*Cast thy bread upon the waters: for thou shalt find it after
many days.*   —*Eccl. 11:1*

A BOTTLE of fine perfume came to me from a friend in a foreign country. The bottle was in the form of a Chinese Buddha and was encased in a shrine-like box with little doors which opened. Its loveliness was too great. I hoarded it.

One day I stepped into the house and was greeted by a fragrance beyond this world. It was springtime. It was the scent of all the flowers that ever bloomed. Unable to locate it, I finally went upstairs. There on the dresser stood the little bottle empty. The perfume had been spilled all over the dresser. It was gone. Gone was my chance to share my treasure with others.

Life is based on the principle of sharing. The sun shares its warmth, the earth shares its wealth, birds share their songs. All nature shares its life, or it stagnates and dies. Man also must share his life to live. If he cuts himself off from the stream of mankind about him, he loses his own life.

Shared treasures are like the bread cast upon the waters. They act two ways. They bless others, and they bless us as well. If we hoard the good things which are ours, we will lose them. If we hoard our love, it will vanish.

Gracious Father, teach me the beauty of sharing my life with others.

Your Gift

The kingdom of heaven is as a man travelling into a far country, who called his servants, and delivered unto them his goods. And unto one he gave five talents, to another two, and to another one; to every man according to his several ability; and straightway took his journey.   —Matt. 25:14-15

A MOTHER surrounded by her children sat on a hillside in the springtime. The children gathered wildflowers and brought them to her—all but the youngest, who was a little feebleminded lad. He gathered up a little bunch of sticks and put them into her lap. The mother's heart rejoiced, for the little sticks were as precious to her as the flowers. Both were expressions of love from her children's hearts.

Our Father regards our service to Him in the light of our own individual talents, however large or small they may be. Jesus recognized that all men are not equal. Some are endowed with larger gifts than others. All are loved the same, but all cannot render the same service. Each one is responsible only for his own potential powers.

The important thing to remember is that God expects each one to serve. He must be faithful in the use of his own gift. His work cannot be done by another, however great the powers of that one may be. God has invested His wealth in us. Let us use it according to our ability.

O God, help me never to say, "Because I have only a little, I will do nothing."

The Perfect Gift

Remember the words of the Lord Jesus, how he said, It is more blessed to give than to receive. —Acts 20:35

A MISSIONARY asked a friend for a donation for his work.

"Well," said the friend, "here are five shillings, seeing it is you who are asking."

"No," said the missionary, "I cannot accept the money, seeing it is for me."

"You are right," said the friend, accepting the rebuke. "Here are five pounds, seeing it is for the Lord Jesus."

When we give to others in the name of the Lord Jesus, the whole aspect of our giving is changed. No gift is too small, no gift too large, when given in love for Him. Mary's alabaster box of ointment and the widow's two mites remain the perfect gifts because they were prompted by extravagant love.

> Give as you would if an angel
> Awaited your gift at the door.
> Give as you would if tomorrow
> Found you where giving is o'er.
>
> Give as you would to the Master
> If you met his loving look.
> Give as you would of your substance
> If his hand the offering took.
> —AUTHOR UNKNOWN

Gracious Lord, accept the gift of my heart, my substance, and my service. I would spread Thy kingdom in the world.

Influences

*Be thou an example of the believers, in word, in conversation,
in charity, in spirit, in faith, in purity.* —*I Tim. 4:12*

A PUBLISHER said concerning his work: "We try to think of our books not just as words printed on paper, but influences. A book is worth while, not because of what it says, but because of the change it makes in a reader's life. He ought to be a different man after reading it. That difference is what really matters about the book."

If books are influences, much more should we think of our lives as influences. "None of us liveth to himself." Our lives touch others for good or evil from day to day.

The life of Peter was so representative of his Master that the people of Jerusalem "brought their sick into the streets, and laid them on beds and couches, that at least the shadow of Peter passing by might overshadow some of them." His very shadow brought the healing that caused men to glorify God.

The shadow one casts on the ground is controlled by the sun. Whether we will it or not, our shadow of influence falls on our household, our friends, our neighbors. When the Sun of Righteousness controls our shadow, it is an influence for good. It heals the hurts of others and brings them a sense of God.

O Living Christ, make me aware of the influence my life casts upon others. May it remind them of Thee.

Your Life Speaks

A city that is set on an hill cannot be hid.—Matt. 5:14

MANY YEARS AGO a student came to this country from England. He found Christ, and his life was remarkably changed. Later on an opportunity came for him to return to his home. He decided to say nothing to his family there about his new-found joy, but to let his life speak for itself. After he was home for some time, his brother said to him, "You are changed since you left home. What is it that you have now that you did not have before? Whatever it is, I would like to have it."

Simple goodness in daily living is the most powerful force in the world. Our lives speak louder than our words. They are open books before all men. Simply to be good, to act as you think Jesus would act if He were in your place, is to send out a light that cannot be hid.

If Jesus had left no record of his spoken words, the remembrance of the life He lived would be enough to change men's lives. His deeds of mercy, his concern for all people, his forgiveness of his enemies speak louder than all the words He ever said. His deeds pointed men to God.

My Father, help me to do rather than to speak. May my daily actions reveal my friendship for Thee.

Letters

Therefore I write these things being absent.—II Cor. 13:10

A WOMAN was confined to an iron lung by paralysis of her chest and arms. She found much happiness in the cards and letters sent to her by friends. She longed to scatter the same cheer among other shut-ins. After months of patient effort she mastered the art of writing with her teeth. Now she scatters cheer everywhere.

Paul was a great letter writer. He wrote to encourage his young friends and the churches he had founded on his missionary journeys. Sometimes he dictated his letter. Other times he was proud to say, "I have written unto you with mine own hand." The Christian world today is richer because some of these letters were preserved for us.

Not many people possess the literary skill of Paul. But each of us can send cheery cards and loving notes of appreciation to people who need encouragement. We can remember anniversaries and express sympathy in times of illness, sorrow, and misfortune. We can share joyous experiences in the lives of our friends. We may build a Christian friendship with someone in a foreign land. We may become a link in a world chain for peace.

My Father, use my pen to bring cheer to someone today.

Multiply Yourself

Then pleased it the apostles and elders, with the whole church, to send chosen men of their own company to Antioch with Paul and Barnabas. . . . And they wrote letters by them after this manner. —Acts 15:22-23

ON THE UNITED STATES POST OFFICE in Washington, D. C., is carved the meaning of a letter:

> Messenger of Sympathy and Love
> Servant of Parted Friends
> Consoler of the Lonely
> Bond of the Scattered Family
> Enlarger of the Common Life
> Carrier of News and Knowledge
> Instrument of Trade and Industry
> Promoter of Mutual Acquaintance
> Of Peace and Good Will
> Among Nations.

Letters play an important part in the spreading of good will in the world. They can be instruments of blessing.

Letters and money are alike in their potentiality. They are both an extension of personality. They can go where you wish to be but cannot go. They may become your hands and your feet and your voice. They act in your place. You multiply yourself when you write letters.

Make me a messenger, O Lord, to spread good will in the world. Give me a desire to share with all mankind.

120

Good Impulses

They helped every one his neighbour; and every one said to his brother, Be of good courage.   —Isa. 41:6

A WOMAN who was driving in her car one afternoon had a sudden impulse to go to the house of a friend. Turning in the opposite direction, she drove to her friend's door. She was met by the little granddaughter of the house who begged her to come in quickly. She found her friend lying helpless upon the floor, having suffered a stroke of paralysis.

God often speaks to our hearts by sudden impulse. We have a feeling that we should make a call at the moment, or write a letter, or telephone a friend. It is important to grasp the impulse when it comes and act upon it. God does not always speak again. We may miss our golden moment.

> It isn't the thing you do;
>   It's the thing you leave undone,
> Which gives you a bit of heartache
>   At the setting of the sun.
>
> The tender word forgotten,
>   The letter you did not write,
> The flower you might have sent,
>   Are your haunting ghosts at night.
>   —MARGARET E. SANGSTER

My Father, I thank Thee that Thou dost lead me to do Thy work. Help me never to lose an opportunity when it comes.

Read I Thess. 4:1-12

Love Your Work

Thou hast blessed the work of his hands.—Job 1:10

MANY PEOPLE look upon work as a punishment. They work because they must. They remember Adam's fall in the Garden of Eden. Because he had sinned, he was driven from the garden to till the ground all the days of his life.

God the creator is not idle. He still works. Jesus said, "My Father worketh hitherto, and I work." Our work is made easier when we think that we are working with God.

Work is a blessing. It depends on our attitude of mind whether it is a joy or a burden. When we love it, it strengthens our bodies and develops our minds. It links us with the creative processes of the world.

> If Jesus built a ship
> She would travel trim.
> If Jesus roofed a barn
> No leaks would be left by Him.
> If Jesus planted a garden
> He would make it like Paradise.
> If Jesus did my day's work
> It would delight His Father's eyes.
>
> —AUTHOR UNKNOWN

My Father, give me an understanding of the beauty of labor. Help me to do my best in whatever work I find to do.

Another Time

*And as he reasoned of righteousness, temperance, and judg-
ment to come, Felix trembled, and answered, Go thy way for
this time; when I have a convenient season, I will call for thee.*
                                                    —Acts 24:25

THE PEASANTS of Southern Russia have a story of an old woman
named Babushka. She was at work in her house when the wise
men of the East, led by the star, passed by.

"Come with us," they said, "for we go to seek the Christ."

"Not now," she replied, "for I am not ready to go. By and by
I will follow on."

But when her work was done, the wise men were gone and
the star in the heavens had disappeared.

Procrastination is the road to failure. That was the sin of the
foolish virgins in the Lord's parable. They really intended to
be ready when the bridegroom came. But they put off filling
their lamps. They went to sleep instead. Suddenly at midnight
the bridegroom arrived, and it was too late.

There is a great difference between good intentions and a
good life. A noble thought, an impulse to surrender our will to
God, comes knocking at the door. But it will disturb our plans
if we yield to it now. So we say, "Go thy way for this time;
when I have a convenient season, I will call for thee." It is a
pitiful fact that the convenient season never dawns.

*Gracious Lord, help me to do today what needs to be done in
my home and in my surroundings to make Christ known.*

The Court Jester

Rejoice in the Lord alway: and again I say, Rejoice.—Phil. 4:4

A STORY IS TOLD of a court jester in olden time. He was beloved above all others in the realm because he lifted the burdens of men by his merriment and kindly deeds. When at last they removed his cap and bells at death, men were astonished to see a poor misshapen creature with twisted form and scarred features.

This man had assumed the role of jester to cover up his ugliness and to hide his broken heart. He succeeded so well that all men everywhere were happier because he had lived.

One of the tests of Christian character is whether or not we scatter joy around us. The ones who scatter it farthest are usually the ones who do so in spite of their own heartaches and disappointments. They seem to realize the world's need for relief from its sorrows.

The joy of the Master came out of pain, but it had a strange healing power for the hearts of men. "That my joy might remain in you, and that your joy might be full." That kind of joy comes back to ease the burden of the heart that sends it forth.

It is not always easy to give a smile or speak a cheery word when the heart is heavy. But it is habit forming. It grows easier by practice.

Gracious Lord, use me this day to scatter joy in Thy name.

Read Gal. 6:7-10

Spreading Happiness

*Let us not be weary in well doing: for in due season we shall
reap, if we faint not.* —Gal. 6:9

WHEN A NEW JUNIOR HIGH SCHOOL was planned, the pupils
urged that it be named for their janitor, whom they called
"Pop." It was a strange idea, for schools in that city were all
named for famous men. But the idea caught on.

"Pop" spent his afternoons and week ends mending broken
skates and bicycles. "He mends teachers' dispositions too," said
one teacher. When asked why the children suggested him, one
girl wrote, "Although it isn't his job to make everybody happy,
he does it anyhow."

"Manners are the happy ways of doing things," said Emerson. "Doing well and happiness are the same thing," said
Aristotle. Graciousness of manner grows out of graciousness
of thought. It expresses appreciation for the little courtesies of
life, and shows affection for those who bestow them.

A girl remarked of her mother, "It was always so beautiful
where mother was." And Wordsworth spoke of

> That best portion of a good man's life,
> His little, nameless, unremembered acts
> Of kindness and of love.

*Jesus, Rose of Sharon, bloom in radiance and love within my
heart.*

Read Rom. 12:9-21

Her Mother's Face

Be kindly affectioned one to another with brotherly love.
—Rom. 12:10

A JAPANESE FAIRY TALE tells of a little girl who looked very much like her mother. The older she grew the greater became the resemblance. One day the mother knew she must go on the journey from which no one returns. She called her little daughter to her and gave her a mirror. She said, "When I am gone, I want you to come each day and look into this mirror. There you will see my face. If you bring smiles, my face will smile back at you. If you bring tears, my face will be full of tears."

After the mother had gone, the little girl came each day to look into the mirror. And always she brought smiles so that her mother's face would smile back at her.

The world gives back to us just about what we give to it. If we give happiness to those around us, we will find it coming back into our own lives. If we speak courageous words, they will return to us in an hour of our own need. If our judgment is kind and generous, others will deal with us in such a manner. When we make an effort to be friendly, we find that friends are waiting to come to us. Should we give only sadness and bitterness, we will find it everywhere about us.

May the brightness of Thy face, O Christ, shine through my life today.

A Merry Laugh

Then was our mouth filled with laughter, and our tongue with singing.   —Ps. 126:2

AT A SUMMER CONFERENCE of young people one of the girls set out for a near-by town to buy a sweater. Later she returned perched high on the hay of a farmer's cart strumming a new guitar. In reply to our questions she said, "Yes, I needed the sweater, but think of the fun we can all have with this guitar."

Years later we welcomed this same girl home from the mission field. Four little girls followed her up the pier. We exclaimed over the four, and she said, "Think of the fun we can have with four instead of one or two!"

This girl always saw the fun in life, and flung out gladness like a song about her.

All of us need to laugh more. We need to laugh at ourselves, at our mistakes and our disappointments—like a person I heard say, "I could have cried, but I laughed instead." Laughter refreshes the heart and relieves the tensions of the day. A bit of merriment, a joke pulled out of the memory or the pocket, often can do more for us than medicine. Have you ever saved up funny little stories and brought them out at mealtime? They are better than a new dish.

Dear Lord, give me the grace to laugh as I go along life's way. Help me to spread happiness instead of gloom.

Trails of Light

Let your light so shine before men, that they may see your good works, and glorify your Father which is in heaven.
—Matt. 5:16

ON SUMMER EVENINGS you may catch your breath as a meteor flashes across the heavens in a shining streak of light.

A lamplighter carried a torch along a city street in days gone by and left behind him a glowing path of light.

If you rise early in the morning, you may see upon the lawn and sidewalks the silver tracings where snails have traveled in the night.

Not many of us are big enough to leave behind us a blazing meteor's trail of light. But most of us can lift a lighted torch and leave the lamps glowing after us. At least we can make a silver tracing on the sand. We are all able to leave the place we occupy a little brighter after we are gone.

Lamps are not made for sunny places. They are made for the dark places of the earth where shame and wrong are found, and for hearts where faith has grown dim and hope is almost gone. These are the places where the Christian's light must shine.

And He once said, who hung on Calvary's tree—
"Ye are the light of the world." . . . Go! . . . Shine—for me.
—AUTHOR UNKNOWN

O Thou, who art the Light of the World, use me to light a path for someone today.

Saints

> Be ye therefore perfect, even as your Father which is in
> heaven is perfect.   —Matt. 5:48

WHY WERE the saints, saints?

> Because they were cheerful when it was hard to be cheerful,
> Patient when it was hard to be patient,
> Because they pushed on when they wished to stand still,
> They kept silent when they wished to talk,
> They were agreeable when they wished to be disagreeable.
> That was all.
>
> —AUTHOR UNKNOWN

Paul called the Christians in the early church saints. They
were saints in the making—as we can be. Jesus never asks the
impossible of us. When He tells us that we must be perfect,
He means that we must make a beginning toward that goal
while we are on this earth. We will finish it in heaven.

If you are a saint, you will not know it. Somebody else will
have to find it out. Sainthood is a by-product of Christian living.
It comes to those who are too busy serving others to recognize
it in themselves.

Someone said, "As we are fast approaching the time when
we shall be called, 'A mean old thing,' or 'A dear old soul,' it
behooves us all to let our joy signals fly now."

*Lead me, O Lord, in my quest for perfection. May the true
graces of the Christian life grow within me.*

"Sunrise and Morning Star"

Be glad in the Lord, and rejoice, ye righteous: and shout for joy, all ye that are upright in heart. —Ps. 32:11

WHEN LUCIFER FELL from heaven, another evil spirit asked him what he missed most from the joys of the celestial city. He replied, "I miss the sound of trumpets in the morning." Do we hear trumpets in the morning?

> Sunrise and Morning Star,
>   And one clear call to give,
> And may there be no clouding of the sky
>   When I go forth to live.
> But such a glow as, shining, seems ablaze,
>   Too full for shade or night,
> When that which drew from out the sun's vast rays
>   Bursts into light.
>
> Daylight and Morning Bell,
>   And after that to work;
> And may there be no soft and subtle spell
>   To make me shirk.
> For though into the maze of toil and strife
>   My tasks may set my way,
> I hope to meet my Master, life to life,
>   As I shall live this day.
>
> —WILLIAM HIRAM FOULKES

Dear Lord, may I face each new morning with a spirit which soars. May I catch its challenge to finer living.

Living Eternally

Jesus said unto her, I am the resurrection, and the life: he that believeth in me, though he were dead, yet shall he live: And whosoever liveth and believeth in me shall never die.

—John 11:25-26

"I am alive forever!"
  This is the word He said;
In Him there is no dying,
  In Him there are no dead;
"I am alive forever!"—
  This is His word to me,
Through springtime after springtime
  To live eternally.

—RALPH SPAULDING CUSHMAN

DEATH COULD NOT EXIST in the presence of Jesus. When He met it on the highway at Nain, it released its hold upon the widow's son. When he approached it at the bed of Jairus' little daughter, she opened her eyes and sat up. When He challenged it before the grave of Lazarus, the doors of the tomb opened and Lazarus walked forth.

Jesus' presence always meant life. He will be with us when we prepare to leave this earth, and He will open for us the gates of life. We shall be alive forever!

O Christ of God, I shall no longer fear death because Thou hast conquered it.

131

Nothing to Fear

*Thanks be to God, which giveth us the victory through our
Lord Jesus Christ.*   *—I Cor. 15:57*

IF WE ARE mature in heart, we meet the experience of death in
two ways. First, we face it. When a loved one is taken, we
courageously realize that we cannot alter the fact by refusing
to believe it or acting as if it is not so. Second, we accept it.
We recognize that it is an experience as natural as birth, that
it is another upward step in a growing life. We rejoice in the
promotion of our loved one.

We find comfort for our temporary loss in the rich memories
that remain with us. They can inspire us to better living and
higher endeavor. We find comfort also in the influences for
good which the loved one left behind. They will go on in
widening circles to bless the lives of those who knew him.

Death need not frighten us when it touches a loved one or
threatens our own lives.

> There is nothing to trouble any heart,
>   Nothing to hurt at all!
> Death is only a quiet door
>   In an old wall.
>
> —NANCY BYRD TURNER

*O gracious Lord, when I stand beside the open grave may I
hear Thy voice saying, "Because I live, ye shall live also."*

A Safe Crossing

*Yea, though I walk through the valley of the shadow of death,
I will fear no evil: for thou art with me; thy rod and thy staff
they comfort me.   —Ps.23:4*

A THREE-YEAR-OLD BOY made a game of going to bed each
night in a different room from the night before. After he went
to sleep, his father picked him up and placed him in his own
little bed. In the morning he awoke in the familiar surroundings of his room.

The limp, unconscious body of the little boy carried in the
strong arms of a loving father typifies for us the experience of
death. We are in our Father's keeping, and we have nothing to
fear.

The ancient Greeks thought that the River Styx had to be
crossed to reach the regions of the dead. The word Styx comes
from a verb meaning to hate or to loathe. Death was an experience to fear and to hate. But when Jesus came, He took
away that dread. He established a bridgehead over that river
and made a safe crossing for Himself and for all those who
follow Him. On the other side He prepared a home and waits
to receive us. When we wake in the morning, we will find ourselves in familiar surroundings and with those we love about us.

*Jesus, Saviour, pilot me over life's tempestuous sea, and bring
me to a safe harbor in Thy heavenly kingdom.*

Coronation

Precious in the sight of the Lord is the death of his saints.
—Ps. 116:15

A SPEAKER opened a memorial service with the words, "We have not come to a funeral service today; we have come to a coronation."

A coronation ceremony is a time of celebration and rejoicing among the subjects of a kingdom. It is an occasion of solemn and holy significance to the sovereign as he assumes his inheritance and enters upon a new and greater life. Amid pageantry and music his reign begins.

We may well liken the passing of a faithful soul into the larger life as such an occasion. It is a time of rejoicing. Pain yields to sweet release. The infirmities of the passing years are gone. It is a time of triumph. The trials of earth are ended. It is a time that is precious in the sight of the Lord.

Think of—
Stepping on shore, and finding it Heaven!
Of taking hold of a hand, and finding it God's hand;
Of breathing a new air, and finding it celestial air;
Of feeling invigorated, and finding it immortality;
Of passing from storm and tempest to an unbroken calm;
Of waking up, and finding it Home.

—AUTHOR UNKNOWN

Triumphant Lord, may I never love the robes of mourning. Give me instead robes fit for a coronation.

Heaven

In my Father's house are many mansions: if it were not so,
I would have told you. I go to prepare a place for you.

—John 14:2

A BOY traveling west on a transcontinental train was telling of the new home to which he and his mother were going.

"How do you know you will like it?" someone asked.

"Father is there getting it ready for us," the boy replied. "I can always trust Father."

We think of heaven in many ways. Jesus spoke of it to the thief on the cross as paradise. The original meaning of this word is a garden or park. A park is a place of lawns and trees, birds and flowers, winding paths and streams—a place where fellowship is sweet. John spoke of it as a city of shining streets and pearly gates, the concourse of all nations. Jesus gave us the best-loved picture of all when he spoke of heaven as a home where the Father is waiting to welcome His children. The loved ones are there; the intimacies of loving companionship are restored once more. There is security there, and no more sorrow, sickness, or sin.

Our Father's house is waiting for us. Jesus has gone ahead to make everything ready for our coming. We may trust Him that when the journey is over He will be there to welcome us.

My Father, I thank Thee that Thou hast prepared a home for me wherein is everlasting joy.

"Good Morning!"

As they went to tell his disciples, behold, Jesus met them, saying, All hail. And they came and held him by the feet, and worshipped him.   —Matt. 28:9

EDGAR J. GOODSPEED uses the words "Good morning" instead of "All hail" in his translation of this passage of scripture. They give new meaning to the Easter scene.

Mary of Magdala and the other Mary hurried to the garden tomb on the first day of the week. The sun was just rising over the mountains; the dewdrops were glistening on the blades of grass; the birds were stirring in their nests. It was morning in the garden.

Suddenly an earthquake shook the ground. An angel rolled away the stone from the door of the tomb and sat upon it. He announced that Jesus was alive and would meet His disciples in Galilee.

Morning dawned in the hearts of these two women. Their night of darkness and doubt fled away. In great joy they ran to tell His other disciples. As they went the risen Lord met them and said to them, "Good morning!" Was ever such a greeting as this!

Some day the eternal morning will break upon our eyes. We shall see our blessed Lord and hear His voice as He says to us, "Good morning!"

Heavenly Father, may I rejoice to know that loved ones wait to greet me in the morning.

Forever Climbing

There shall be no night there; and they need no candle, neither light of the sun; for the Lord God giveth them light: and they shall reign for ever and ever.   —*Rev. 22:5*

LESLIE WEATHERHEAD tells of finding somewhere in an old church yard one of the loveliest epitaphs he ever read: "When we saw the glory of his sun-setting, we said, 'It will be a lovely day tomorrow.'"

Clement of Alexandria, an early church father, said, "Christ turned our sunsets into sunrises."

The glory of life on this earth is primarily achievement in growth of character, and in service to our fellow men. Surely this will carry over into the other life. We shall continue to climb higher in spiritual development. We shall progress by means of our service to others. The place in which we serve does not greatly matter. God uses us for His glory both in this world and in the next.

Let us think of our loved ones who have gone as ever advancing in wisdom and experience. Let us see our brave young lads who leave us in early manhood as ever climbing far heights, forever joyous, forever free.

Loving Father, help me to banish my loneliness by dwelling upon the glories of my loved ones who have gone into Thy nearer presence.

Holding Them Back

O death, where is thy sting? O grave, where is thy victory?
                                          —I Cor. 15:55

IN AN EDITORIAL Arthur Brisbane tells of a company of caterpillars carrying an empty cocoon to its burial place. The caterpillars were dressed in black and weeping sadly. All the while above their heads floated the butterfly on bright wings, rejoicing in its new freedom and life.

The poet Grace Noll Crowell has given us the thought that only when we rejoice in the freedom of the one who has been released from the limitations of the earthly life can that one "explore unhindered the sparkling meadows of eternity." Our selfish grief, she says, tends to hold him back from the freedom he has won—

> For how can I go on while your hearts are breaking?
> There is a golden light on the land ahead;
> The winds are cool and sweet, I am strong for climbing,
>   I am not dead!

Our clutching hands must let go of the dear ones who pass beyond our sight. We must give them back willingly into the keeping of God, trusting that He has better things for them than we can give. Only then shall we know peace.

Dear Father, help me to dwell upon the glory of the passing of my loved one to God rather than upon my own loss. Forbid that I should hold him back from the joy he has won.

138

Comfort

Blessed be God, even the Father of our Lord Jesus Christ, the Father of mercies, and the God of all comfort; who comforteth us in all our tribulation, that we may be able to comfort them which are in any trouble, by the comfort wherewith we ourselves are comforted of God.   —II Cor. 1:3-4

IN *Pilgrim's Progress*, Christian and Hopeful come to a river that is the final barrier to the City of God. As Christian wades into the current, he is all but overwhelmed. But Hopeful says, "Be of good cheer, my brother. I feel the bottom, and it is good."

Comfort must be more than soothing words. It must express the root meaning of the word: *con,* "together"; *fortis,* "strong" —two joined together in strength. Comfort comes only when one can say, "I too was about to be swept away, but I found a safe footing. So can you." It is worth going through deep waters if we can do that for another. It is one of the compensations for our griefs. God replaces our losses with the priceless gift of bringing hope to others.

> Give other friends your lighted face,
>   The laughter of the years:
> I come to crave a greater grace—
>   Bring me your tears!
>
> —EDWIN MARKHAM

Gracious Father, I offer Thee my broken heart to use in binding up the sorrows of others.

God and the Dirty Dishes

*For I the Lord thy God will hold thy right hand, saying unto
thee, Fear not; I will help thee.*   —Isa. 41:13

AT THE CLOSE of an evening meal I asked my little son to stay
with me for a while. He complied, but soon he heard the call
of a playmate outside.

"If you go, I shall be lonely," I said.

"No," he replied, "you will not be lonely. You will still have
God and the dirty dishes."

God and the dirty dishes! I wondered at these words. Are
they not the two answers to our cry of loneliness and sorrow in
every Gethsemane of our hearts?

God is forever with us, the beloved Companion and Com-
forter. In every house of distress He abides when all else goes.
His presence can mean more to us than any human relationship.

And the dirty dishes still wait to be washed. Such familiar,
homely duties remain to be attended to. They hold within
themselves healing for the broken heart. Christian service calls
for loving hands and dedicated minds. We find our comfort in
giving ourselves afresh each day to tasks for Him.

*Father, grant that I may find this day the work Thou hast
for me to do. May I continue all day long with a sense of Thy
presence.*

Hope Restored

For thou art my hope, O Lord God: thou art my trust from my youth.

—Ps. 71:5

HELEN HAYES lost her beautiful young daughter Mary from polio. Her heart froze within her, and she could not speak her daughter's name. One day a woman named Mrs. Isaac Frantz, who had just lost a little son from polio, came to see her. It took great courage for her to ask to see a celebrated star of many Broadway plays.

Mrs. Frantz told Miss Hayes of her plan to adopt an orphan from Israel. Miss Hayes was shocked.

"You are thinking I am letting him take my little boy's place?" Mrs. Frantz said. "No one could ever do that. But in my heart there is still love, and maybe wisdom, too. Should I let these dry up and go to waste? No, my dear, we cannot die because our children die. I should not love less because the one I loved is gone—but more should I love because my heart knows the suffering of others."

Helen Hayes knew her own search for God was ended. She found Him through the human heart of this humble woman. Hope came back. She realized that, although Mary was gone, she herself was a better person for having hoped and dreamed and worked for her. It was tragic that Mary's life should have ended, but how much better than if it had never existed.

Forgive me, O Father, if my losses have blinded me from Thee. Help me to continue to hope in Thee.

Past Sorrows

And Joseph called the name of the firstborn Manasseh: For God, said he, hath made me forget all my toil.—Gen. 41:51

JOSEPH WAS A MAN who in maturity had learned the secret of forgetting past sorrows and forgiving past injuries. He named his first son Manasseh, which means one who causes to forget. Joseph was able with God's help to forget his tragic past: the unhappiness of his childhood, the treachery of his brothers, the loss of his parental home, the years of slavery and imprisonment in a foreign land. Nothing could ever change these things, so he put them behind him. He cleared his life for present and future achievements. He made it possible for God to bring good out of evil.

It is deadly to brood over the sorrows of the past. Drop the habit here and now. Open your mind and heart to the sunshine of the present. God will fill it with new blessings.

> Every day is a fresh beginning,
>   Every morn is the world made new.
> You who are weary of sorrow and sinning,
>   Here is a beautiful hope for you,—
>   A hope for me and a hope for you.
>   —SUSAN COOLIDGE

Grant me, O Lord, strength to forget and to forgive. Help me to close the door upon past sorrows.

A Second Chance

And the word of the Lord came unto Jonah the second time.
—Jonah 3:1

WHEN MY LITTLE GRANDSON was born, one of the startling joys that came to me was the thought that God was giving me a second chance. He was giving me another opportunity to help mold a new life for Him. However I might have succeeded or failed in the past, here was a chance to do better.

God is always doing that for his children. God told Jonah to go to a certain city to preach. But Jonah didn't want to go, and ran in another direction. After he had paid the penalty for his disobedience, God called him again and gave him a second chance.

We ought to be looking for these second chances. They are all around us. It is never too late to grasp them.

> He came to my desk with a quivering lip—
> The lesson was done—
> "Dear teacher, I want a new leaf," he said;
> "I have spoiled this one."
> In place of the leaf so stained and blotted,
> I gave him a new one all unspotted,
> And into his sad eyes smiled—
> "Do better now, my child."
>
> —KATHLEEN WHEELER

God of the second chance, grant me power to build upon my failures of the past.

Living Memorials

Thine alms are had in remembrance in the sight of God.
—Acts 10:31

A FATHER AND MOTHER lost their young son in a tragic accident. They desired to give a memorial to him. They owned a house in a city where there were two theological schools. They remodeled the entire upper floor and made apartments in it. These they rent to young theological students with families for one fourth the cost they would pay elsewhere. Thus they contribute year after year to the training of young ministers in the name of their son.

Monuments of stone remind us of the past with its loss and grief. They serve no helpful purpose for the living.

Living memorials are reminders of life instead of death. They may serve to carry out the life purpose of the one who has gone. A mother said, "I will endow a scholarship for a mountain boy who has no opportunity for a Christian education, in memory of my son who was a teacher."

We find our hearts strangely comforted when we know someone else is carrying on in the place of one we love. We know that the influence of that life will live on in other lives to bless the world.

Grant, O Lord, that I may remember my loved ones by serving others in their name.

Anniversaries

I have remembrance of thee in my prayers night and day.
                                        —II Tim. 1:3

A JAPANESE GIRL eight years of age lost her only sister in a traffic accident. She determined to do something about it. She saved her money until she had enough to have a number of small handbills printed. Then she stood on a corner of a busy street in Tokyo amid the traffic and gave them out to passers-by. The handbills said, "Because I lost my sister in a traffic accident, I know how the family of the victim feels. So I am asking you to be careful as you drive in traffic." Each year in June, on the anniversary of the accident, she hands out these bills. She distributes as many as ten thousand each year.

Anniversaries of losses are difficult to bear. The sense of loss returns and saddens the heart. The victorious Christian finds a way out. He may observe the day of memory by acts of helpfulness and gratitude.

On the anniversary of the death of a fine lad his mother said, "Today I shall be especially thankful because it is the anniversary of his entrance into the Father's house. I shall rejoice for him and show my gratitude by helping others for his sake."

Give me strength, O God, to observe the anniversary of my loss by an act of gratitude and love. Help me to complete some unfinished task of the one I love.

Nothing That Matters Is Gone

The mercy of the Lord is from everlasting to everlasting upon them that fear him, and his righteousness unto children's children. —Ps. 103:17

A BOY went with his grandfather to the site of the old family home in Nebraska. All that was left were a few stones of the foundation in a tangle of weeds.

"Here is where the house stood," said the grandfather. "Here was a picket fence. There were lilac bushes and peonies, and over yonder the barn. There were thirteen children who played here."

The boy could scarcely believe they were ever there. The grandfather could not believe they were gone.

"All gone, aren't they, Grandfather?" said the child.

"Nothing that matters is gone," the grandfather answered.

We can never lose the things that really matter in life. We can never lose the heritage of a fine family, the memory of a good father and mother, of loyal brothers and sisters. The things they gave us are a part of us forever. We can never lose the wealth we find through the reading of great books and through travel. We can never lose fine friendships. Nothing can ever change the glory of God's beautiful world. It is made new every day for our enjoyment. Everything that really matters is ours forever.

My Father, I thank Thee for the wealth that no one can take from me. I am rich in the things that really count.

Forgetting the Past Mistakes

This one thing I do, forgetting those things which are behind, and reaching forth unto those things which are before, I press toward the mark for the prize of the high calling of God in Christ Jesus.   —Phil. 3:13-14

THEMISTOCLES, the Greek philosopher, said, "Teach me the art of forgetting; for I remember what I would not, and cannot forget what I would." Themistocles lived in a pagan world, and he did not know where to turn to learn to forget. Paul knew this art from his understanding of the Master. Of all men Paul had reason to regret his past. He had persecuted and slain the followers of his Master. The memory might have haunted him forever. Instead he thrust it behind him and fixed his eyes upon Jesus and pressed on.

Everyone makes mistakes. When we recognize them and ask forgiveness for them, we should forget them. Regret is useless unless it brings repentance, and repentance is worthless unless it brings reparation. When this is done, let go of the mistakes forever.

Take God with you into the days ahead. His name is Emmanuel. It means "God with us." His strength will reinforce yours. He will keep you from falling. "He will hold you fast."

Dear Lord, who art always ready to forgive my mistakes, help me to forgive myself also. I would forget the failures of the past.

147

Old Friendships

A man that hath friends must shew himself friendly.
—Prov. 18:24

Beautiful and rich is an old friendship,
Grateful to the touch as ancient ivory,
Smooth as aged wine, or sheen of tapestry
Where light has lingered, intimate and long.

Full of tears and warm is an old friendship,
That asks no longer deeds of gallantry,
Or any deed at all—save that the friend shall be
Alive and breathing somewhere, like a song.

—EUNICE TIETJENS

As THE YEARS PASS, we realize more clearly the value of old friends. They bring us comfort and joy no others can give. They know us for what we are. They share our memories of the past. They understand our hearts.

True friendship must be earned. It must be treasured, and it must be kept in repair. There must be an interchange of messages and of hours spent together. Our friend must know that our feeling for him is still warm and tender.

Silence, indifference, and neglect will kill this priceless treasure. Hold on to your friendships. They are one of God's best gifts.

I thank Thee, O Father, for old friendships. Help me to treasure them.

Light from Above

The Son of man is as a man taking a far journey, who left his house, and gave authority to his servants, and to every man his work.   *—Mark 13:34*

A GREAT ART GALLERY has no windows in the walls. One reason is that the walls are needed for paintings. But the chief reason is that the pictures must be lighted from above to bring out their beauty. The world is lighted from above, and the artist tries to show us things as they are. Therefore the windows of the gallery are placed in the roof.

The average person thinks of life as a commonplace affair. He can see no particular reason for his existence. Life is just the same old round of work and sleep with nothing grand and beautiful about it. He is dominated by a desire to achieve things which add only to his temporal enjoyment. He fails to find any of the spiritual values in life.

That sort of person needs to throw open the windows of his soul and let in the light of heaven. He needs to find God's plan and purpose for life. Every person may experience the touch of God's hand upon his life. Every person may be conscious of being used of God in some worth-while task.

When we view life in the light from above, we find that its real treasures are spiritual. We discover that God has a purpose for us which will add new dignity and beauty to it.

O God, let me be conscious of Thy plan for me each day. Use me in some worth-while task today.

Treasures of the Darkness

The darkness hideth not from thee; but the night shineth as the day: the darkness and the light are both alike to thee.
—Ps. 139:12

NIGHT-BLOOMING JASMINE blossoms in the month of September. After darkness falls, the tiny white trumpetlike blossoms open and unearthly fragrance fills the air. The perfume fades with the daylight. Only darkness calls it forth.

God speaks to us through his prophet: "I will give thee the treasures of darkness, and hidden riches of secret places, that thou mayest know that I, the Lord, which call thee by thy name, am the God of Israel." We learn many things only when we walk through the shadows. Sometimes that is the only time that God can get our ears. When we suffer pain or loneliness, material things fall into second place. Spiritual values become the real ones. We can hear God's voice better in the darkness than in the light.

> Why do I creep along the heavenly way
>   By inches in the garish day?
> Last night when darkening clouds did round me lower
>   I strode whole leagues in one short hour!
>
> —AUTHOR UNKNOWN

Kind Father, when shadows fall upon my life, help me to discover some hidden treasure in them. Help me to find Thy presence there with me.

New Values

While we look not at the things which are seen, but at the things which are not seen: for the things which are seen are temporal; but the things which are not seen are eternal.
                                        —*II Cor. 4:18*

IN A POEM called "The Strange Medical Experience of Karshish" Robert Browning tells of an Arab physician who visited Lazarus in Bethany after Jesus had raised him from the dead. He tells that Lazarus has a new and strange attitude toward things. His values appear entirely different.

> Speak of some trifling fact,—he will gaze rapt
> With stupor at its very littleness,
> (Far as I see) as if in that indeed
> He caught prodigious import, whole results.

If we could but possess the wisdom of the other world, if we could see as God sees, we would have an entirely new set of values. We would see with different eyes. Many things we think are important would mean very little to us. Things we call trivial would become large in meaning.

Jesus expressed this truth in many ways: "He that is greatest among you shall be your servant." "Whosoever shall not receive the kingdom of God as a little child shall in no wise enter therein." "He that loseth his life for my sake shall find it."

Correct my values, O Father, that I may not miss the true meaning of life.

Possessing All Things

As sorrowful, yet alway rejoicing; as poor, yet making many rich; as having nothing, and yet possessing all things.
—II Cor. 6:10

AFTER THE EARTHQUAKE in Long Beach, California, in 1933 we moved from our two-story house into the garage. In one large room we set up our bed, the children's beds, and a few necessary pieces of furniture. Housekeeping was simple. We had what we actually needed; we were safe; we were happy because we had one another. That was what really mattered.

"What do you want me to give you for your birthday?" a little girl said to her mother.

"Just give me a kiss," replied the mother. "Then I'll not have to dust it."

A person may have few material possessions and yet be happy. As we grow older, we find we do not need many things we once thought we did. We find that they add to our cares. The pleasure we find in youth in collecting many things may become the joy of giving them away in later life.

We need never fear poverty. God has promised to supply all we need. We may say with the psalmist, "The Lord will give grace and glory: no good thing will he withhold from them that walk uprightly."

Lord of all, I bless Thy name that Thou dost supply my every need. I am not afraid of any lack.

Glory, Hallelujah!

Grow in grace, and in the knowledge of our Lord and Saviour Jesus Christ. To him be glory both now and for ever.
—II Pet. 3:18

POLIO ROBBED a young man of the use of his limbs. He walks now by the help of two crutches. He has printed on one crutch the word "Glory" and on the other the word "Hallelujah." His face is shining and his spirit is triumphant. He looks upon his infirmity as an opportunity for new adventures with God in growth and in faith.

Our heavenly Father desires his children to be perfect in body and in mind and in spirit. He wants them to grow continually toward this ideal. Because we live in the kind of world we do, there are obstacles to overcome and limitations to conquer. The physical body is subject to decay. But in the realm of the spirit, growth is forever possible. Bodily infirmities have no power to touch the spirit. They may even enrich the spirit with new strength and beauty.

If we are deprived of the activity of former years, we may have more time for the things of the spirit. If there seems no relief from pain, there may be opportunity to grow in patience and in understanding. When a blessing is lost, we may find another and a greater one to take its place if we look for it.

I will look today, my Father, for Thy new blessing to fill the vacant places in my life.

153

New Year

Lord, thou hast been our dwelling place in all generations. Before the mountains were brought forth, or ever thou hadst formed the earth and the world, even from everlasting to everlasting, thou art God. —Ps. 90:1-2

As NEW YEAR'S EVE draws on toward the midnight hour, a hush of expectancy seems to cover all the earth. It creeps into every heart. Something old is about to die. A chapter of life is ready to close. Something new is about to appear. What does it hold for you and me?

This sense of expectancy is characteristic of youth. The young person is impatient to experience life. He runs to meet it. As we grow older, we do well to hold on to this attitude. Change is the only certain thing in life. It is good, not evil. It is the thing which enables us to grow if we meet it with expectancy and a sense of opportunity.

God knows when we are ready for a change in our lives. He brings it about that we may be stimulated to bigger and better experiences. If we meet it with faith and trust and an abiding sense of His goodness, we will not fear the unknown. Years do not matter. We may be young in spirit and greet the future with a song.

Dear Lord, I cannot see what lies ahead in the new year.

*I only know Thou lovest me
And Thou wilt lead me on.*

Easter

That I may know him, and the power of his resurrection.
                                                    —Phil. 3:10

> For resurrection living
>   There is resurrection power,
> And the praise and prayer of trusting
>   May glorify each hour.
> For common days are holy
>   And year's an Easter-tide
> To those who with the living Lord
>   In living faith abide.
>
> —AUTHOR UNKNOWN

THE DISCIPLES OF JESUS were transformed when they realized that He had survived death and was still with them. They entered upon a new experience in their lives, which we might call "resurrection living." Their faces were set toward the sunrise. Strength and grace were in their hearts. Praise was upon their lips. Power was in their actions.

Resurrection living may be your experience and mine. When the fear of death is removed from our hearts, there is nothing else left to fear. We can never lose our loved ones. We shall continue to learn and to grow eternally. Life is not limited to one world. Richer, vaster experiences await us in the world to come.

Heavenly Father, may the splendor of the resurrected life be mine today.

Mother's Day

In thee, O Lord, do I put my trust.—Ps. 31:1

LIFE WAS NEVER EASY for my mother. At the age of four she stood upon a chair before the sink to wash dishes for hired help in the field. Throughout a long life she knew her share of hard work, and of affliction and disappointment. She never traveled outside the community in which she lived. Her name was never mentioned in print.

She was a Christian woman, rich, mature, and glorious. Her face shone with an inner radiance. Her spirit was brave because she put her trust in God. She left her children a shining example of the love of God in a humble life.

> Today I heard a song from out the air.
> I think it came from heaven, or somewhere
> That voices chant of sweet, ecstatic things,
> I know that on this day my Mother sings.
>
> Today I heard a song from out the past.
> 'Twas of another childhood gained at last.
> Through all the tender beauty this day brings,
> I know, beyond the skies, my Mother sings.
>
> —MED RANSOM

Dear Father, may the memory of my mother lead me closer to Thee.

Thanksgiving Day

Sing forth the honour of his name: make his praise glorious.
—Ps. 66:2

THE THANKSGIVING HABIT is a healthy one. It opens the door for communion with the Author of everlasting mercy and the Giver of all good gifts. It cleanses the soul of selfishness. It releases the spirit from depression and fretfulness. Gratitude is the payment of a debt we owe to God.

> One midnight, deep in starlight still,
> I dreamed that I received this bill:
> ———— in account with Life:
> Five thousand breathless dawns all new;
> Five thousand flowers fresh in dew;
> Five thousand sunsets wrapped in gold;
> One million snowflakes served ice-cold;
> Five quiet friends, one baby's love;
> One white-mad sea with clouds above;
> One hundred music-haunted dreams,
> Of moon-drenched roads and hurrying streams,
> Of prophesying winds and trees,
> Of silent stars and browsing bees;
> One June night in a fragrant wood;
> One heart that loved and understood.
> I wondered when I waked at day,
> How—how in God's name—I could pay.
>
> —CORTLANDT W. SAYRES

For all Thy mercies, O Lord, I thank Thee.

Christmas

And when they had opened their treasures, they presented unto him gifts; gold, and frankincense, and myrrh.

—Matt. 2:11

TRUE CHRISTMAS GIVING comes from the heart rather than the purse. It finds expression in gifts not always found in the merchandise marts of the world. Often they have no material value at all. They are gifts of faith and love and cheer. They feed the spirit and last when all other kinds are gone.

> O, I would celebrate my Lord
> With every gift my means afford,
> And I would wreath His name around
> With every joy I ever found,
> And I would light a candled tree
> For everyone on earth to see,
> And I would stand all night to bake
> For every hungry soul a cake,
> And I would send a star to greet
> My brother soul on every street,
> And I would sing my love among
> The carolers in every tongue,
> And I would wish at last to be
> On Christmas Day as poor as He.
>
> —JEAN KENYON MACKENZIE

O holy Child of Bethlehem, teach me to give as Thou dost give.

SOURCES OF QUOTATIONS

Acknowledgment is gratefully expressed to the persons and organizations, indicated by asterisks (*), who have given permission to quote selections.

PAGE — REFERENCE

10 G. H. Palmer, *Life of Alice Freeman Palmer.* Houghton Mifflin Co.

21 Carol Barnes, "The Jon Lindbergh Story," in *This Week,* Feb. 8, 1953.

31 Ellinor L. Norcross, "Devotions," in *The Christian Century.**

32 E. Stanley Jones, *The Way,* p. 267. Abingdon-Cokesbury Press.*

34 Lynn J. Radcliffe, *Making Prayer Real,* p. 40. Abingdon-Cokesbury Press.*

39 Ethel Romig Fuller,* "Proof."

46 Suggested by leaflet *For Shut-Ins Only.* The United Prayer Tower, St. Paul, Minnesota.

47 Mary Alice and Maurice Flint, *The Story of Your Mustard Seed Remembrancer.* Flint Co., Kansas City, Missouri.

54 Albert Schweitzer, *Out of My Life and Thought.* Henry Holt & Co.

56 Roy Meredith, *The Face of Robert E. Lee in Life and Legend,* p. 137. Charles Scribner's Sons.

59 Rebecca McCann, *The Complete Cheerful Cherub.* Copyright 1932 by Covici, Friede, Inc. Crown Publishers, Inc.*

60 Helen Keller,* "In the Garden of the Lord." Doubleday & Company, Inc.*

61 Edwin Markham, "Victory in Defeat." (By permission of the author's son.)

62 Karl Kohrs, "I'm Glad I'm Homely," in *Parade,* Oct. 7, 1951.

73 Estelle C. Carver, *Meditations and Plans for the Quiet Day,* Oct. 25-31, 1950. Woman's Division of Christian Service of The Methodist Church.

78 Fanny Heaslip Lea,* "Bomber's Moon," in *Good Housekeeping,* Aug., 1943.

92 Dwight Farnham, *A Place in the Country,* p. 193. Funk & Wagnalls Co.

93 Luther Burbank, *The Harvest of Years,* p. 11. Houghton Mifflin Co.

102 E. Stanley Jones, *Victorious Living,* p. 329. Abingdon-Cokesbury Press.*

109 John Masefield, "The Everlasting Mercy." Copyright 1930. The Macmillan Co.*

124 Annie Fellows Johnston, *The Jester's Sword.* L. C. Page & Co.

126 Teresa P. Williston, "The Mirror of Matsuyama," in *Japanese Fairy Tales.* Rand McNally & Co.

130 William Hiram Foulkes,* "Sunrise and Morning Star."

131 Ralph Spaulding Cushman, "Easter," in *Spiritual Hilltops.* Copyright 1932 by Ralph S. Cushman. Abingdon-Cokesbury Press.*

132 Nancy Byrd Turner, "Death Is a Door," in *Star in a Well.* Copyright 1935 by Dodd, Mead & Co., Inc.*

138 Grace Noll Crowell,* "To Those Left Behind."

139 Edwin Markham, "Your Tears." (By permission of the author's son.)

141 Helen Hayes, "In My Darkest Hour—Hope," in *Reader's Digest,* Mar., 1952.

146 Marguerite Harmon Bro, *Every Day a Prayer,* pp. 247-48. Willett, Clark & Co.

148 Eunice Tietjens, "Old Friendship," in *Leaves in Windy Weather.* Alfred A. Knopf, Inc.*

158 Jean Kenyon Mackenzie, "My Christmas Wish," in *Glowing Ember,* compiled by Catherine McAfee Parker. Board of Foreign Missions, Presbyterian Church, U.S.A.*

159

Index

DATE DUE

242
Emm   Emmons, Helen B.
      The mature heart

9503008